A Crying Game

A. Crying Game

The diary of a battered wife

JANINE · TURNER

MAINSTREAM
PUBLISHING

First edition published in 1984 by
MAINSTREAM PUBLISHING
25 S.W. Thistle Street Lane
EDINBURGH EH2 1EW

ISBN 0 906391 49 0 (casebound)
ISBN 0 906391 52 0 (paperback)

Typeset by Spectrum Printing Company, Edinburgh
Printed and bound in Great Britain by
Billing & Sons Ltd., Worcester

This is not a work of fiction

Acknowledgements

I would like to thank: Jackie Henrie (Editor) my guide, mentor, and friend; Erica Jong for permission to use extracts from her book: *How to Save Your Own Life*; Peggy Seeger for permission to use her song *Emily*, © Ewan MacColl, Ltd. This song is available on HOT BLAST (BR 1059). Blackthorne Records, 35 Stanley Avenue, Beckenham, Kent BR3 2PU. Chris Rogers for giving her time so willingly and at such short notice; Scottish Women's Aid staff for all their help and support; all those who gave their time and patience to answer my many questions; and Mike for his support and encouragement.

And a very special thank you to Gill and Boyd for looking after Joanne so well. I couldn't have done it without you!

Thank you all.

Janine Turner

CONTENTS

*the Lady of
Shalott!*

Foreword

Again the voice spake unto me:
'Thou art so steeped in misery,
Surely 'twere better not to be'.
ALFRED LORD TENNYSON

"Have a cup of tea . . ." A cup of tea . . . a cup of tea. The words echo and re-echo around my mind. The room begins to blur. The figure before me fades. Suddenly, I am back in the past. A cloak of darkness covers me completely. I escape beneath its folds, glad of a reprieve.

It is a sweet, syrupy darkness, cloying, claustrophobic. Here, I feel safe. From what, I am not sure. I don't know. I don't care. All I want to do is sleep. I snuggle down, and it is as if the blackness around me closes in.

Someone shakes my shoulder. "Have a cup of tea," they coax.

"Leave me alone, leave me alone," I cry. My throat feels thick, my mouth dry. I try to crawl back into the blackness, but They won't let me. Something warm touches my cheek. I cling to it for comfort, as a child would a favourite doll. But it struggles free. My arm is gripped in a vice, and from far away I can vaguely hear a voice urging me to sit up. All right, all right, I will. Maybe then They will leave me in peace.

The cold rim of a cup is pressed to my lips. Warm liquid runs down my chin and on to my chest. I push it away weakly with a hand that doesn't seem to belong to me. But They are persistent. They try again. Sweet tea fills my mouth. It tastes good. But I don't want to drink . . . I want to sleep.

I open my eyes. Light stabs them and I wince. A flash of white comes towards me and I shrink back, instinctively afraid. Afraid of what? Someone bends over me, plumps my pillows, straightens the bedclothes, fussing . . . fussing . . . fussing. More tea follows, scalding my throat.

Things become clearer. I look down to see my body floating before me. My feet are out of focus. It is an effort to move. I feel light-headed. I turn to look for the figure prowling around my bed. "Where . . . where am I? What's the matter?"

My husband's voice scorches across the covers, "You silly bitch. We can't call a doctor. There would be too many awkward questions."

Questions crowd my mind. Then suddenly I know. *I have no need to ask. I need to face the awful truth. I had tried to take my own life—and failed.*

The preceding episode cannot be dated. Its actual time of happening has been totally blanked out by the author's subconscious. The author wrote this book through regression, and to use her words: 'It wasn't easy. I wrote it through regression—by reliving the past to feel again the hurt, the rejection, the utter hopelessness of being nothing. It was a shock afterwards to return to the present. I felt I had to write it this way. It recalled my deepest feelings of the time, so that I am able to tell my story as it was and not how I remember it. The experience has been of great therapeutic value; putting my life down on paper has helped me to come to terms with myself.'

Emily

Once we were single, once we were young and
Once we were happy, husband and wife,
But fourteen years married, thirteen years harried,
Now I don't care what comes of my life.

The first time he lifted his hand against me,
He knew the blow was hurtful and wrong,
He put his arms round me and said he was sorry,
Sorry love, sorry, all the night long.

The next time he lifted his fist against me,
I thought I'd provoked him, I was to blame,
The next time, the next time and the time after,
I told no-one 'cause I was ashamed.

If anything crossed him, I got his fist,
If dinner was late he slapped me around,
With stitches and bleeding, begging and pleading,
Nothing would do till I'm on the ground.

My mum come round, she seen I was cryin',
Seen I was cut and bruised round the eyes,
My husband turned round, all smilin' and charmin',
Says "All she does is spend and tell lies."

He said I was out with men every day,
He locked me indoors and tore up my clothes,
My friend heard me screaming, never come near,
Why did I stay with him? God only knows.

If I go quiet, that makes him rage,
If I turn and run, he's hunting me down,

I says, "Why do you hit me?" He hit me for asking,
Whatever I do, I'm down on the ground.

Each afternoon my heart would start trembling
I followed his journey all the way home,
His step at the door would nearly dissolve me,
When he walked in, my judgment was come.

I know there's two sides to every question,
I may be wrong and he may be right,
But he's got just two ways to settle a quarrel,
One is his left, the other his right.

The doctor says he needs my understanding,
The police seldom challenge a man in his home,
Everyone knows him, no-one defends me,
After the altar, a wife's on her own.

I wander, I cry, I pray I may die,
I run up to strangers to talk in the road,
Three kids and no money, so how can I leave him?
I lose my kids if I've got no home.

Sometimes he's loving, sometimes he's caring,
Sometimes it seems our marriage may mend—
And then in the night I'm lying and wondering,
How soon will his fists be at me again?

The last time he hit me, he nearly killed me,
I thought I was dead and glad to be free,
I gathered the kids up and went to a refuge,
He grabbed a crowbar and come after me.

When I go out, I see him behind me,
Three times we've moved, he's found us again,
If I kill myself, at least I'll die easy,
At least I'll know why, at least I'll know when.

The refuge is bare, the floors and walls echo,
Nothing reminds me of comfort or home,
But here I can sleep and here I can hope,
Here I have friends, I'm no longer alone.

Peggy Seeger

INTRODUCTION

Battered Women—Some Facts and Figures

Throughout history women have been beaten by their husbands or partners and no-one thought such violence was anything to get worked up about. A wife was a man's chattel in exactly the same way as a cooking pot or a piece of furniture—his to do with as he pleased. It was considered to be a man's right to beat his chattel if she failed to live up to his expectations. Over the centuries men have been conditioned within the home and educated outwith the home to believe in and fulfil the role of master. Physical violence is one means by which they can reinforce this role and exercise their control over their women. Women, on the other hand, have always been regarded as men's subordinates—and, in many cases, servants—and this has been reinforced by society at every turn.

It was not until the 19th century that some attempt was made in Britain to prevent wife beating. In 1853, an Act was passed which made a husband, convicted of assaulting his wife, liable to a maximum fine of £20 or six months in prison. Such an assault was, of course, hard to prove and a conviction difficult to obtain. In this country the right of a husband to beat his wife was not completely abolished until 1891. However, despite this, the beatings continued, and still do.

Violence against women was only really brought out into the open in the 1970s when women all over the world began to join together to fight for their rights. They campaigned against many abuses, domestic violence included, to which women were subjected.

People everywhere began to recognise the fact that no matter what the argument between a man and his partner, there is no justification for him beating her, and that something had to be done

11

to help women who were suffering at the hands of their violent men. Thus the very first refuge was opened in 1971 by Chiswick Women's Aid. From then on Women's Aid grew, until today there are refuges and offices throughout Britain.

In 1974 the House of Commons appointed a Select Committee on Violence in Marriage to investigate and report back on the problem of domestic violence against women and their children. One of their recommendations the following year was that there should be 500 refuge places in Scotland alone. Unfortunately this has yet to happen. At the time of writing there are just over 100 refuge places in Scotland; England has over 200 refuges; Northern Ireland 5 refuges; and Wales 20 refuges.

The statistics concerning battered women are alarming. In Scotland in the year 1982-83 960 battered women and 1705 children were accommodated in refuges, but a staggering 1605 women had to be turned away due to lack of space. In Wales 883 women and 1405 children were accommodated; no records are available of those who had to be turned away. In Northern Ireland 600 women and 1300 children were accommodated, but space could not be found for 250 women. Unfortunately Women's Aid Federation England are in the process of compiling their statistics and could not give us any comparative figures at present.

Domestic violence is surrounded by many misconceptions. One popularly-held opinion is that domestic violence occurs only in the lower classes of society, but this is not at all the case. Men who batter their wives come from all walks of life—they can be labourers, skilled tradesmen, social workers, teachers, doctors, dentists, lawyers. There is no class distinction whatsoever.

The degree of physical violence used ranges from slapping, kicking and attempted strangulation to burning with lighted cigarettes and other forms of torture. According to research carried out in Scottish cities in 1974 by Drs Rebecca and Russell Dobash, sociologists at Stirling University, the second most common violent offence in Scotland is wife assault.

Mental cruelty can be every bit as damaging as physical violence. It can include preventing a woman from going out on her own or seeing friends, continually telling her she is ugly or stupid, or not allowing her any money of her own.

Another popular misconception is that a woman must enjoy being treated violently, because if she didn't she would leave. The truth is that many women would like to leave, but instead they stay with their violent men because they find the alternatives that present themselves in the world outside the marital home too frightening to contemplate. They are often too ashamed of being beaten to talk about it to anyone, whether it be doctor or friend. They do not know where they could go if they did leave. Often such women do not know that Women's Aid exists. The idea of approaching a solicitor for advice terrifies them. As for the DHSS—the very word conjures up untold humiliation. They worry about how they would manage financially and, if they have children, they worry about how the children would cope with the disruption to their lives that leaving home would cause.

In our society marriage is still seen by many as the goal towards which all women should aim. Therefore many women believe that to leave a marriage is to be seen as a failure as a woman. The percentage of women who leave and then later return to their men is high. In fact last year in Scotland alone 46% of women accommodated in refuges returned to their violent partners. (No figures are available for England, Ireland or Wales). It is likely that much of the reason for this large percentage is that the odds are quite simply stacked against these women: refuges are not for long term stays; DHSS rates are subsistence level only; council houses are often difficult to obtain and of low standard and minus home comforts when women are eventually offered them.

But what of the women who are determined to stay away and make new lives for themselves and/or their children? Women's Aid will give them advice and temporary accommodation in a refuge if they require it. The refuges are run on self-help lines. The women staying there decide for themselves how to run the household. Men are not allowed and refuge addresses are kept secret to prevent violent men from seeking out their partners. Children too are accommodated with their mothers and their needs catered for at what for them is a very traumatic time in their lives. Thus through Women's Aid a battered woman can have a breathing space in which to come to a decision as to what to do next—a decision no-one can or will make for her. If she decides to stay away permanently from her violent man, Women's Aid will help her in every way—with housing, DHSS, solicitors, etc. They also run a follow-up support service for women who have left the refuges and act as an information service about legal rights, welfare benefits, etc, for all women.

The law too does not give sufficient protection to women. The police should be encouraged to take a more direct approach to domestic violence. As the Parliamentary Select Committee on Violence in Marriage pointed out in 1975:

'We believe that effective police intervention in the area of domestic violence would do a great deal to reduce the problem of violence in this country.'

At present the police are often reluctant to intervene in domestic disputes, just as women are often reluctant to press charges of assault against the men with whom they are living.

It is my firm belief that until both large-scale re-education of the sexes is carried out, and the law is changed with stiff penalties imposed for domestic violence, men will continue to beat their partners. How long should this violence be allowed to go on?

Jackie Henrie

1956-73

Life can only be understood backwards, but it must be lived forwards.
                    SÖREN AABY KIERKEGAARD

1956
A child toddling in the rose-filled garden. Cornfields. The common. Laughing, playing, walking, running. Running? Crying. One foot drags behind the other, hampered by the iron rod reaching up her leg. At night, another rod clamps her feet together in a frozen embrace. Calipers.

A head of copper-coloured curls bobs up and down in the wind. I can hear the wind. I can feel the wind. Mummy, why can't I see the wind?

Questions, questions. Always questions.

I see myself. Yesterday's child. My mother beckons from the bungalow. Dreaded Thursday. Weekly hospital visit. Green railings —small hands gripping them tight. A constant crying game. A child's voice screaming, scrabbling to break free from hands that hold. White coats. White plaster. White sterile walls. Endless corridors. The clump, clump, clump of one-legged men walking up and down, down and up. And hands, pricking, prodding, poking.

The grating whine of a drill. Two brown eyes brim with tears as the saw moves to and fro, cuts open plaster. A dusty leg, weak and sore and thin. Tears, cuddles, kisses. Waiting, interminable waiting, watching those one-legged men and wondering . . . Then the slap and tickle of sticky bandages and plaster of paris sealing up my leg. And the donkey ride and cake in a café after to make it all

15

better . . . until next time.

1961
Talk of operations. Tears. Trust in words of comfort. A corner bed. Crisp, cold, cotton sheets. Waiting and watching in the dark, trying desperately to understand. Injections. White gowns and caps. Masked faces peering down at me. Walls closing in to smother me. Men . . . people? Figures in green coats and wellies. Hurting . . .

Waking to see a long low hump in the bed. Peering beneath the covers at where my leg should be and seeing instead a cage. Panic. Confusion. Screams. Shouts.

Children. Nurses. Doctors. Rosemary, my doll, clutched tight. Another plaster encasing my leg. Shaky hand scrawling a letter:

> *Dear Mummy,*
>   *I love you very very much and please please please please PLEASE I want to come home with you.*

1962
Easter. Move to South Wiltshire. Dad becomes a minister. Little village school. I creak up the aisle in my hospital shoes to read prayers in assembly. Readings. Scripture. *Mill on the Floss, Silas Marner.*

'Come on, girl. You of all people should understand the Lord's Prayer. Your father's a minister.'

1963
Move to South Wiltshire. Housing Estate. Unhappy. Moody. School bullies.

'Have you heard the latest by The Monkees?'

'Oh yeah. It's the greatest, isn't it?'

'What's it called, then?'

'Er . . .'

Mad dash home to gen up on The Monkees for the next day.

'Come cycling.'

'Come to the Locarno, ice skating.'

'I can't . . . I can't . . . I can't!'

'Why not?'

'I've got a bad leg.'

'Janine's got a bad leg, Janine's got a bad leg,' becomes the new school chant.

Hospital again. Plaster cast. Broken ankle roller skating. Trying to keep in with the crowd.

Home from school via the cake shop. Comfort food. Midnight feasts to allay worries about school. Exams. Down in physics, down in maths, down in chemistry, down . . . down . . . down . . .

Piano lessons. Clarinet, Recorder. Music! Escape into fantasy. Illusion. Dreams about the future. Family concerts in the church hall—reality.

1967

Move to Northampton. New beginnings. First pair of shoes. Girls' school. Picnics in the park. Class of nine. Catching up on lessons. Catching up on friends. The past is gone. Forget the past. Singing in the church choir. Concerts at hospitals and OAP Clubs.

'Have you seen that Dave?'

'No. But I had a fantastic time with Greg last night.'

'Mmmm. He's dishy. What about you, Jan? Who do you go out with?'

Boys. Boys? What do I know? Me! Who's never had a date! Always the odd one out. Church meetings. Church outings. Church concerts. Church choir practice. Music . . . and cakes.

1969

Move to D_____. Thoughts about college. University. Teacher Training. Music. R.E. Bible College? Bible Coll . . .? No! No! No! No college does music. Back to school on one condition—I have to join a lower class, kids two years my junior.

A crash of brick breaking glass. A jagged hole in the classroom window. Someone scribbles 'Janine did it' across the blackboard. Enter teacher. The chant begins:

17

'Janine did it . . . Janine did it . . . Janine did it.'

'Who broke the window?'

'Janine did, Sir.'

Thirty-nine out of forty say she did.

'Look, I'm sorry to have to do this. But what else can I do? You can see how it is . . .'

Detention. For something I never did.

A gaggle of girls giggle at a group of boys across the way. Skirts hitched up as high as regulations will allow. Perfume bottles do the rounds. Eyes gummed up and hair fluffed out. Swaying hips, legs long and tantalising in dark-coloured tights. A scene from *West Side Story*? Perhaps. But with me playing the lead. As they move around in a circle the spotlight is on me.

'SSSSsssss,' they hiss, like serpents about to strike.

I recoil in fear.

'Ja . . . nine, Ja . . . nine, Ja . . . nine.'

The teacher on playground duty retreats to the staff room for coffee.

'She wants to have sex . . . she wants to be kissed . . . she wants a boy . . .' They test me. Tantalise me. Taunt me.

In class, my chair is kicked from under me. My books scribbled on. I confide in 'a friend' only to find she is a traitor. A game of cat and mouse ensues. And I am being baited into the trap.

1970

A dark January evening. I hurry home from choir practice. A shadow dogs my footsteps. I walk quicker. It walks quicker. I walk faster. It walks faster. A figure appears at my side. The voice whispers into my ear, 'Shall I carry your bag?'

I ignore the approach.

'Are you shy, or something? What's the matter with you?' An arm winds itself around my shoulders. I wriggle away.

'Come on, now. Loosen up a little, lady.'

'Leave me alone, can't you?'

We approach the corner and I turn for the first time to face him.

'What's all this about? What do you want?'

'Naïve, aren't we?'

Then he kisses me in the full light of a street lamp. I freeze.

'Want to go to the pictures?'

Now outside my gate, the light from the window gives me courage. 'Would you like to come in and meet my parents? Have a coffee or something?'

'You what?'

The figure disappears rapidly down the darkened street. Six months of worry follow. Am I pregnant from the encounter and the kiss?

I meet Bill in the Church Youth Club. He goes out of his way to be nice. He takes an interest in me. I don't really like him to begin with, but when he joins the RAF it makes him more adult in my eyes. A man. When he turns up on my doorstep one evening, I grudgingly invite him in. I am watching an old film on TV. He wriggles and squirms in a chair until my parents suggest I take him in the other room to listen to the radio. Under protest, I give in.

'Why don't you come and sit by me?'

I decline.

'Mind if I smoke?'

It's cold. He snuggles his RAF coat around my shoulders. I remember the war hero doing the same to his sweetheart and I find myself playing the part. I slide shyly next to him on the sofa to receive my first real kiss.

To me, he is a man of the world. He tells me how he is ridiculed at the camp, hounded by the authorities, always given extra duties for having dirty boots or not shaving. He is an outcast. Different. We identify with one another.

My life turns upside-down then, becoming a series of 'highs' and 'lows'. I call it 'Love'. I spend long evenings by the phone, willing it to ring. When it does, I crawl inside.

'I'm sorry, love. I won't be home for your birthday like I promised. I've been put on jankers again for dirty boots and long hair on parade . . .'

'I'm sorry, love. My forty-eight hour pass is cancelled. I don't know why. Could be something to do with not ironing my kit properly . . .'

'I'm sorry, love. . . .'
'I'm sorry, love. . . .'
But when he does get leave and meets me outside school how I love the way everyone stares and comments on the handsome RAF uniform waiting for me at the gate!

'Dishonourable Discharge' from the RAF.
'Too good for them,' he boasts and sets about finding a flat. All I can think about is finding him a good home and being together.

We find him a bedsit in the centre of town. I take a book-keeping job at a shop, and every evening after work, I hurry back there to prepare a meal. He returns from the factory, changes, eats, and disappears into the night. In his absence, I wash his clothes, clean his room, tidy his wardrobe. Later I sit reading romances of how love should be. Waiting.

The roar of a motorbike heralds his return.
'Still here? Well, you can go now . . . Mummy! Billy's home like a good boy, and he's going to bed.' His voice taunts me as I run to catch the last bus home. But next day, I'm back for more, always hoping that this time it will be different.

1972

The landlord stands solidly at the foot of the stairs. 'You can tell your boyfriend he's out. He's not paid the rent in a month, and you can clean the place before you go. Do yourself a favour. Find yourself a real man.'

I race up ahead of him. The sink is full of vomit. Beer bottles lie about the floor. Clothes collect dust in a corner. I gather them up and put them away. In the wardrobe I find a pair of size twelve tights and bra. Not mine. Later I confront him with them.

'Oh, I bought them ages ago as a present for you. I wasn't sure if they were the right size so I opened them. They weren't, so I pushed them to the back of the wardrobe. No harm in that, is there?'

Bill is quick to defend his actions. Has he someone else? What does he do when I go home? Where does he disappear to after dinner? I do not voice my suspicions. I dare not question for fear of losing him. And we leave it at that.

'I don't like him, pet. Why don't you find someone better?'
'Look at the way he's treating you! There are plenty more fish in the sea.'
Mum and Dad make their feelings clear.
'Bring her home by ten.'
'Spend the night in with us playing a game.'
They seem to be deliberately forcing us apart. I resent their interference. I can make up my own mind about things . . . and be right! I'll prove it. They have made all my decisions for me. Now it's my turn.

Bill finds digs with a lady who puts up boys from Borstal and men looking for homes. I begin work as a Child-care Assistant, live-in, at a Children's Home some seven or eight miles away. It is now his turn to visit me. I give him money for petrol and a drink across at the pub while I finish my spell of duty.

1973
We meet outside the Home.
'Come on, let's go for a drink.'
'I'd rather stay in tonight and do something together.'
'Oh, don't be such a bore!'
'Look, why do we always do things you want to do and never seem to take into account my feelings?'
'Little Miss High and Mighty is it now?' By now an all too familiar scene.
'Give me some money then, and I'll go out and leave you alone?'
'No.'
His hand leaves a burning streak down my cheek.
'I haven't got enough to last the week as it is.'
'Sod that!'
His hands feel hard and merciless as they hit me around the head. In trying to duck out of his way, I trip over a stone. I fall to the ground.

'Take that, you tight-fisted bitch!' His foot kicks where it hurts.

'Bill? Bill stop it! You're hurting! People are looking at us!'

A couple across the road pass as if with their eyes shut. It could have been an everyday occurrence. He leaves me where I have fallen. I watch his long legs carry him on down the street.

'Bill? Bill . . . wait for me.'

For one fleeting moment, I think of going home. But Bill seems the only chance I have of breaking free, of being free. I catch him up at the crossroads and together we walk into the pub.

He buys me a long cold lager to make up. It tastes bitter. Two packets of crisps and four packets of peanuts later he leaves to buy a box of my favourite chocolates from the shop.

'Here you are then. Don't say I never buy you anything.' He is pleased with himself for thinking of it. I try not to worry about it being my money that he's spent and how I'll last till payday.

The Children's Home has put on a party for my twentieth birthday. We put the children to bed as usual then congregate in the hall for cake and drinks. Bill arrives late and tipsy. Bangs toy drums, belts bedroom doors, creates havoc, annoyed that the party is coming to a close. Children wake, confused, crying at the noise. Bill flakes out just as the crying and confusion reach a peak.

I feel ashamed. He is my responsibility. I can't apologise enough.

'Why don't you leave him, Jan? He's a real louse.'

'Better the devil I know than the devil I don't,' I try to shrug off the tension.

The truth is, I'm scared—scared of being alone again, scared of making a new relationship, scared of simply being Me. Everyone has someone else. Two halves of a whole. Bill is my passport to life, to freedom.

Where would I be without Bill?

1974

To name oneself is the first act of both the poet and the revolutionary. When we take away the right to an individual name, we symbolically take away the right to be an individual. Immigration officials did this to refugees; husbands routinely do it to wives.

ERICA JONG

19 January 1974
The day was cool and crisp, the sky clear and blue. A perfect day for a wedding.

'Janine, will you take Bill to be your lawful wedded husband? Will you love him, comfort him, honour and keep him in sickness and in health, as long as you both shall live?'

My father's voice reverberated around the packed church. People stood still and silent, as if holding their breath for the final words to be spoken. At the back were the children from the Home, out in force, in best bib and tucker. Every now and then, little Mark's voice broke into the proceedings adding the sole note of light relief into the otherwise awesome atmosphere. Bill, at my side, looked nervous. He smiled lopsidedly, mumbling his responses so that his words were lost in his moustache. I wished he'd speak up. I wanted everyone to know that he was accepting his responsibilities like a man.

In the centre of the church stood the bulk of the congregation—people who had known Bill as a boy, and had watched him grow up, the relatives: Aunts and Uncles from all four points of the compass. A real gathering of the clans, who only met at special events like weddings, christenings, and funerals. Soon, they would be gone out of our lives, apart from the odd postcard or birthday greetings.

Ahead of me were the choir, and 'Uncle Harry' standing straight and proud, as if this were his finest hour. Many were the evenings spent with him and Kath sharing my hopes and dreams, philosophising on life. Aware of my inner conflict, my turbulent emotions, they had their doubts about this wedding, but knew I had my own life. Harry gave a secret smile, and linked hands with Kath. A shining example of true love.

Behind me, my two sisters stood like sentries on duty. The youngest, awkward in a long dress, held her posy tight like an Olympic torch and blushed a deep red if anyone looked her way. Jackie was just a child. She and Laura had giggled together in corners all the way through my stormy courtship, keyhole conspirators trying to glimpse their future.

Mum stood as one alone, keeping her anguish private. A sad smile betrayed her role of proud mother. Even at the church door she had been ready to support me should I change my mind. Hoped even? I would prove her wrong, allay her fears.

I had a sudden urge to giggle. My shoulders began to shake and I fiddled with my veil to hide my embarrassment. Tears stung my eyes. I found myself crying. Then I wanted to laugh. What was the matter with me? My emotions were running riot. In the corner of my vision, Bill's left leg trembled to and fro. Formal in tailored suit, he stood like a stranger at my side.

At last, shakily, I spoke the words everyone was waiting to hear. 'I will.'

I held my breath. No thunderbolt exploded from the heavens, no fanfare of trumpets, only heavy silence marked the seriousness of the occasion. Not even Mark provided light relief.

The Wedding March regaled us down the aisle. So this was it. A gold band locked around the third finger of my left hand. Marriage. I caught Mum's eye. She smiled—sadly—and I looked quickly away.

February 1974

No longer living in the Children's Home now that I was a married woman. Bill was working nightshift for extra money, so I found myself alone quite a lot of the time. Long, dark, silent nights. It was always the same. I would lie beneath the covers, clutching a hot water bottle for comfort. It would grow cold. I would consider padding to the kitchen for another, but knew I couldn't do it. I hated being alone. I saw a figure in every shadow, heard an intruder in every rustle. I felt foolish opening and shutting doors, peering petrified into cupboards, but I couldn't help myself. I couldn't sleep as long as there was a chance someone else shared our flat. I couldn't sleep anyway.

Seven until ten o'clock stints at the Children's Home were exhausting, and afterwards, I was fit for nothing but bed. But I knew what to expect when I trudged up to the front door of our flat in the evening. I always dreaded facing the chaos I knew I'd find inside. Bill would have gone to work long since, leaving a trail of havoc marking his departure. There would be a note saying the rent man had called wanting payment, and a conglomeration of dirty dishes, cigarette butts, broken crockery, and beer bottles scattered around the floor.

March 1974
Row to end rows. Sparked off when my engagement ring bent in half, then broke. Bill in a frisky, playful mood had been demonstrating judo techniques picked up in the RAF.

'Well, what do you expect for fifty pence? Diamonds?' He laughed.

'But . . . but I thought . . .'

'You thought what?'

He was taunting me, challenging me, standing over me, hands gripping my shoulders in a vice—shaking, shaking, shaking me until I'd thought my teeth would rattle. Suddenly, he let me go. I fell backwards into a chair. He moved to the other side of the room and sat smoking, watching me out of slit eyes.

My mind went back to the one time we'd called off our engagement. He was still in the bedsit then, and about to make his usual exit after dinner. I asked him to stay. Pleaded with him even, to let us just talk for a change. I was desperate for company.

'I'm fed up with all this waiting around. Be my man. Give me some attention instead of giving it all to drink.'

'You're fed up! I'm sick to death of your whining, woman. Give me that ring, and clear out of here by the time I get back. I don't care if I never see you again.'

Tears of pent-up frustration had blinded me, so that I'd only heard him slam out and stamp down the stairs. I hadn't wanted it to end. I only wished to be wanted, needed, loved. I sat on the bed and finished my latest romance novel, then took him at his word and 'cleared out'. I took everything I had paid for—food, pots and pans, crockery, cutlery, even clothing. Now he would have to come to me when he wanted something. I knew he had no money. I had only to bide my time until he came. He would need me.

At home, tea and sympathy.

'You're well rid of him. He never did treat you right, pet. Let me make you some tea.'

I wished my parents would say nothing. They meant well, but it made my indecision worse. They didn't know the half of it. But still I was afraid of being alone. My sisters now had boyfriends. Why was I a failure? Why couldn't I make my own relationship work?

At the end of a week, I crept downstairs in the early hours of the morning. I pulled the phone as far as the cord allowed and dialled his number.

'Hello, it's me. Can we meet?'

Silence. I knelt, huddled over the phone. Spoke in whispers so no-one would hear.

'Hello . . . hello?'

'What the hell do you want?'

Not quite the response I was looking for, but at least he'd answered. Another five minutes elapsed. I coaxed and wheedled. Finally he relented grudgingly.

'OK then. I'll meet you by the river tomorrow at noon. But this time we get together on my terms.'

It had sounded like an ultimatum. Nevertheless, I was there, waiting for him like the sucker I was. My original ring had been lost over the past few days. I wondered whether he'd sold it to buy food, but if so I blamed myself. After all, I'd taken everything he had. He bought me another to replace it, and we resumed from where we left off.

Now he was telling me he had paid fifty pence for it.

'Where did you buy it then?'

'From the market, where else? I needed my money for other things.'

I lost my cool then, and used words I'd never even thought of using before. He was dragging me down to his level. I knew it, and I hated him for it. I hardly recognised the harsh, vulgar voice as my own.

Then the blows began.

'You bitch! I'll show you who's boss . . .' He retaliated in the only way he knew how, and I became a punchball. His hands punched my eyes, nose and mouth until they looked a bloodied mess, while a knee buffeted into my stomach. I sank to the floor. A slave kneeling before her master. I felt drained. Desperate. My fingers found a hold. I pulled, punched and kicked, determined not to be beaten. Usually, I kept a low profile. But this time I was so incensed I gave vent to my feelings for the first time in months. My legs bore bruises from the kicks. My stomach was painfully sore. Above all, my pride was hurt. The row ended abruptly when he slammed out of the flat and didn't come back.

I cleaned up and crawled belatedly into bed in the wee small hours of the morning. I was looking forward to the long weekend ahead, but thoughts of what happened earlier kept milling around in my head, would not let me sleep.

A scream rang out, snapping my mind suddenly back to the bedroom. I cowered beneath the sheets. The scream came again, followed by the sound of breaking glass. Voices raised in anger. Then silence resumed. The bangs and thumps began again. Pat and Ray downstairs were having a fight of their own. It seemed to be the area for it. I turned over and buried my face in the pillow, plugging up my ears, and slept.

I was awakened by something cold and clammy clawing at my clothes. I tried to push it away, but it came in closer. Hot breath panted on to my face, bristly stubble rubbed my cheek, irritating the skin. Fingers sticky with sweat moved down my body.

27

'Bill . . . Bill, is that you?' I tried to get a hold, but my arms were pinioned to the mattress.

'Stop it, Bill. You're scaring me.' I became a writhing, wriggling worm, working my way to the floor.

'Wazzat?'

He was drunk. A hand reached down, feeling, searching, stabbing. I lashed out like a tormented tigress—clawing, clinging, scratching.

'Unfreeze, ice-maiden. I'm going to get what's due. It's time I had some fun.'

He found, held, hurt.

I felt used like a whore, a prostitute, someone he'd picked up off the streets. This was brutal, rough. This was Rape. It made me feel unclean. A scream rang out into the night. This time, it was me. It came from within. I didn't expect it not to hurt. It always had. It always would, as far as I was concerned. I just thought it should be somehow different. Books I read made it out to be so much more than it was. But then books always did that. Bill was the only person I had ever had sex with. He led. I took my cue from him. He taught me all I needed to know. He hurt.

Things got better after that. They always did for a while, as if lulling me into a false sense of security. Until the next time. I began to believe life was on the up and up, that Bill had reformed. He was sorry for that night of terror. He had been drunk, hadn't known what he'd been doing. On bended knee, he asked forgiveness, and I forgave. Besides, I blamed it on the way we were living. It would be different when the Council gave us a house. And I blamed myself. I always blamed myself.

May 1974

Our love has been put to the test several times over, these past months, and it is hard to believe there can be any harder test waiting for us in the future. Yet this has to be, for we cannot pick the rose without the thorn. Much as we would love life always to be bright and beautiful, we need the bad and the ugly to help us appreciate what we do have all the more.

9 June 1974
Bill arrested.

We had both retired to bed early for once, in celebration of the end of the three-day week. I was trying to overcome my fears of being touched, and had just begun to untense a little when there was a pounding on the front door. Bill went to answer it. He came back to dress, looking somewhat sheepish.

'I have to go to the station. Don't worry, I'll be back soon.'

'The station . . . ?' I hadn't quite come to grips with the situation.

'Yes—the Police Station. I'm being booked.'

'Wait a minute. I'm coming with you.'

The next couple of hours were spent listening to an account of how he and two friends had been joy-riding in a stolen car. Bill had been driving, and he was the one who had been caught. Now they needed the names of his accomplices.

It was a change to see him wriggling under pressure. He cowed in the face of authority, pleading with them to keep his name out of it if he 'grassed'.

'We'll see what we can do—Sir. Now then, you were saying . . .'

16 June 1974
Burgled. My guitar was the only thing to be taken. I was shattered. It was my one escape. My one means of keeping sane. I felt alone without it. Bill became nervy, edgy, started staying in more than before. I was grateful for the company. At last, he understood—I thought. He loved me—I thought. He wanted to make amends for the past—I thought.

23 June 1974
Bill arrived home from work badly beaten up. Visit from police followed. My guitar had been found in a second-hand shop, where it had been hawked by the two accomplices to teach Bill a lesson for 'grassing' on them. He refused to press charges. He had other things on his mind. Police wanted to take him into custody for non-payment of a forty-pound fine. I was still living in Cloud Cuckoo Land. I bailed him out of trouble with the forty-pound cheque I had

just received from work.

'I'll pay you back, Jan—honest I will! You're a real gem.'

The money went out on permanent loan.

1 July 1974

Dear Mum and Dad,

Thanks for putting up with us over the weekend. It was wonderful to get away for a while. I'd loved it to have been longer—a lot longer.

I wish you could understand how I feel. I know I have hurt you by marrying Bill. But I have never gone against you before in my life. And in this I still feel right. It hasn't been easy. But then, I never thought it would be. With him I have grown up. I am a woman now. I have experienced life. We have our arguments, but doesn't everyone?

Please try to understand. Accept me for what I am. It would mean so much. . . .

Still I strove to justify my existence.

4 July 1974

My twenty-first birthday. I expected to feel different, things to change. But life went on as normal. We held a party to celebrate, but it rapidly became a boozy affair, with Bill and a couple of friends taking centre stage. My sisters and the couple from the ground-floor flat left early. I sat. My mince pies, pasties and cake turned to crumbs. Beer bottles piled up on the floor. I sat some more. Then I went to bed.

12 August 1974

a.m.

Just saved my first hundred in the bank, after weeks of going without tights, meals, treats. It was a proud moment for me as I entered my last three pounds on the white giro slip and handed it over the counter with the notes.

p.m.

Bill found my cheque book. Demanded I give him the money to buy a car he'd seen, and added a few well-aimed kicks for good measure. His boot reached up to thud into my bottom. I turned and yelped, an animal in pain, as he cracked my knee. It gave under me. I fell to the floor. 'There'll be more where that came from if you don't.' His words held a note of menace.

13 August 1974

I was so proud of my bank balance, and the way it had mounted up slowly over the weeks. I couldn't let it go now. I simply couldn't. I kept out of his way all day. Left for work early, and arrived home late. But he was waiting.

'Don't say I didn't warn you.'

I found out the hard way that it was best not to show it hurt. If I screamed or shouted with pain he'd do it all the more. I felt like an animal being tortured, just to see how I would react.

'Bill. Stop it,' I screamed, as he batted my head against the wall. Each time it made contact I thought it would be my last before I passed out. A fisted ball punched the air out of my stomach. Vomit came up in my throat.

'Bi . . . ll!' I choked on his name.

He didn't say a word. His fists and feet said it for him. I gritted my teeth. Swallowed painfully. Dug nails into the palms of my hands until they raised blood. Anything to take my mind off the agony of it all. Only when he was gone, had run off, would I cry.

14 August 1974

I wished I hadn't tried to be brave the previous night. Now I had the additional shame of walking down the street with a black eye. I kept in the shadows. Turned my face to the wall. But still people stopped and stared.

'You've been in the wars, haven't you? What did the other fella look like?' The cashier peered closer, as I stammered something about walking into a door.

Bill had a smug smile on his face as I meekly handed over the money that night. I couldn't bite my tongue. 'But what's the point of buying a car when you can't even drive?'

A stinging slap caught me on the side of the cheek.

'I can take lessons, can't I? Now shut up, woman. Who are you to tell me what to do?'

He left without another word.

15 August 1974

5.30 a.m. My pillow was so wet with tears, I could have wrung it out. I looked for signs of a car outside, that might be ours—correction, His—but there was none. Puzzled, I went to put on the kettle. The fridge was stacked full of beer cans. I found Bill on the sofa in the front room. The remains of a Chinese take-away splattered the carpet. His sleeping fingers still held a cigarette butt. It had burned holes in the cushions, dropped ash on the floor. I knelt to take it from him—and he woke.

His glazed eyes stared at me as if I were a stranger. I searched for that spark of love that must be there, somewhere, but decided he was still suffering from the after-effects of drink. Then slowly, he focused on me, and smiled. I was overwhelmed. A ray of sunshine broke through my despondency. A glimmer of hope began to grow. I clung on to it as I leaned forward to hug him.

He pushed me away roughly, and pointed to a corner of the room.

'See. See what I bought? I had a real ball last night.' Almost two dozen rock records lay by the stereo. Hundreds of cigarettes were neatly stacked in two piles beside them. On top was a box of chocolates. My reward? 'Have one, if you like.' He looked proudly over his possessions, while I choked back the tears. I had cried enough. I was just one more possession he had grown tired of.

'What happened to the car?'

'Oh that, I changed my mind didn't I?' He was like a child who had been given too much pocket-money to spend.

'Anything left, any change?' I queried, hopefully.

He laughed. 'Never give up, do you? Only enough to buy my mates a beer or two at dinner.'

I hesitated for a moment before asking my next question. 'What about work, then?'

But he had an answer to that, too. 'It's raining outside, or hadn't you noticed?' He never went to work in wet weather if he could help it.

'Lend me some bus fare, will you?'

I turned around abruptly, and left for work, slamming the door hard behind me.

6.45 a.m. A wall of noise hit me as I stepped through the door. Then silence.

'Hi, Sal,' I greeted the night nurse.

'Morning, Jan. Like a cuppa?'

I appreciated the tea, smiling ruefully as the bedroom antics began again.

'Been like this since six,' said Sal, striding towards the nursery unit of the Children's Home.

'Hey!' Her raucous voice echoed around the walls. 'That's enough!'

'It's OK. I'll go in to them,' I suggested timidly.

'Right then, I'm off. Bye.'

Sal never looked back. The outside doors swung shut behind her. I felt trapped.

'Anni Jan.' That was Michael. Baby Michael. One and a half years. There were some compensations.

'Anni Jan . . . ?'

I took a deep breath, opened the door, and plunged into another day.

The room was a mess.

'Darren! What do you think you're doing?'

Darren stood and stared. Baby blue eyes chose to ignore the neat pile of screws in one corner, his collapsed cot in the other. The nuts and bolts expert. Three years old.

'Linda, come away from the window! Phil, put away those books. Mary, pull Graham back out from under the bed, there's a good girl . . .'

Stop the world. I want to get off . . .

8 a.m. We had reached the breakfast stage.

'Dick, please try to concentrate. Put some egg on your fork . . . that's it. Good boy. Now, hold your head over your plate and . . .

No!'

Yellow yolk splattered on the wall. Dick giggled. He was a spastic. Twelve years old with a mental age of three. I suppose he tried. Paul, up in his high chair, decided to follow his example. Soon, egg was flying in all directions. I picked out a blob from my hair and cleared the plates.

Playtime. We adjourned to the main hall where a slide, a rocking horse, various forms of plastic transport, and a box of toys waited to be abused. Mary and Jean had left for school with the others. I worried about them like a mother. But they were tough. They had to be to survive. Their mother was a prostitute.

I stepped back into the nursery, mechanically clearing, washing, drying dishes. Sorting, mending, making beds with envelope corners.

'Don't you say anyfink 'bout my Dad, you fucker! He's the best, he is. . . .' Words of abuse hurtled to and fro outside. I hurried back to the hall.

'Mark! Stop it . . . stop it. You'll hurt him.' I grabbed an arm and leg from the tangle of bodies writhing on the floor, dragging free the kicking, screaming, shouting boy.

'He called me a liar. He said my Dad was . . .'

'Mark . . . Mark . . .'

We fought our way back through the bedroom door and fell on to the first bed we came to. I rocked the frustrated figure to and fro on my lap.

'He didn't mean it. He doesn't know,' I soothed, stroking the sandy-coloured hair. He cried then, hiding his face in my lap. His father was in prison. His mother couldn't cope. He was being penalised by his friends. They didn't understand about his hard-headed exterior being a front to hide the deep, deep hurt he felt inside.

11 a.m. Coffee break. I cleared a path to a seat and sat down for the first time in two hours. Orange was passed around to the children. They munched happily on biscuits. Dick, the spastic, sat cross-legged on the floor playing with his willy through a hole in his trousers. His shriek of laughter made some of the girls giggle. His

laugh was infectious. His face baby smooth, naïve, innocent.

My head ached. I touched the lump at the back tenderly. I remembered the night before. A bruise was turning black on my arm. I pulled on a jumper to hide the evidence.

'Coming to the party tonight, Jan?' Neil asked on his way past.

Yes, yes, yes. I'd love to come.

'No. I'd better get home. Bill will . . .'

'Bill. . . ? Ugh!'

He looked as if he had a bad taste in his mouth as he passed through the swing doors into the sunshine. My knee throbbed in sympathy.

1.00 p.m. Dinner was beefburgers and chips. The children's favourite. They clamoured for more. I tried not to notice the way Mary's knife and fork formed a cross on the table. She was praying. Michael watched anxiously from the sidelines. Brother and sister, they were devout Roman Catholics. The others teased them about their faith. Their mother had died only recently, and aware of their great loss, I treated them like fragile dolls.

'Mary . . . have some pudding,' I chided gently. She raised her head. Our eyes met. I felt strangely disquieted by her direct approach.

'Dick! Now no more mess, mind.' I turned my attention elsewhere.

I took them for a walk in the park. Michael and Paul sat in the twin pushchair. Darren held one side, Dick the other. Mark romped ahead to let everyone know we were coming.

'Push me, Anni Jan.'

'Lift me on the roundabout.'

'Tell Michael to stop kicking!'

It was chaos. Bedlam. They went mad. I went mad inside.

'Give the boy back his ball, Mark. It isn't yours.'

'Come on. Come and get it, weakling! Or I'll thump you where it hurts.' Mark's bullying voice sent the boy crying to his mother.

'Cry baby . . . Cry baby bunting.'

The boy's mother was furious. She channelled her anger at me. 'Look here, if you have to have this many kids, at least keep them in order.'

She stormed away out of the park.

'Sorry, Aunty Jan. I . . .'

'I know, Mark. I know. Come on, everyone. It's time to go.' Red-faced, I hustled my brood down the road, back to the Children's Home.

'One, two, three . . . Where's Mark? Four, five . . .' I counted heads.

I took a roundabout route, stopping at the shop for sweets. We passed the bus stop and I watched curiously as a woman leapt ahead of us. A bus pulled up. I expected her to get on board. Instead, she dragged Darren from the pushchair . . . and ran.

'It's all right, all right, all right,' I calmed the panicking children.

Should I leave them and give chase? I saw her jump with the boy on to the bus. I moved in pursuit.

An arm pushed me off the bus and I thudded back against the wall of the shelter. It jarred my already bruised body. I felt sick. The bus moved away out of sight.

'Come on, all of you.' I walked them back and near to tears reported the incident. It had been on the cards that Darren's mother would try to take him back. Proceedings had already begun to get him back into care.

4.30 p.m. Jam sandwiches and cake for tea. Even Dick managed admirably on his own. I took a breather and two paracetamols to kill the throb in my arm and head.

'Jan? Can you get another cot ready? We've a late arrival.'

The children sat happily in the television room as I unfolded sheets and set up the cot.

'Jan. . . ?'

I took the bundle that was handed to me. Pam, the Super-intendent, came to help.

'Found in a phone box,' she explained as we washed and dried the thin crumpled body.

'Poor little mite!'

5.30 p.m. I began to run baths. It had been a long day. My back ached as I bent over Dick, the last of eleven. He was in a playful mood. Water splashed over the side. He kicked, catching my bruised arm. I felt like screaming with the pain.

'Dick! Dick . . . behave.'

He giggled. I left him sitting on the potty in the corner while I checked on the others in the bedroom.

Darren was busy taking his cot to bits again. I jerked it back to the wall and tucked him in for the umpteenth time. Mary wanted to say prayers.

'God bless Daddy. Keep him safe. Don't let him get lonely. God bless Michael and me. And please God, make Mummy happy with you in Heaven.'

A lump caught in my throat. I kissed her tenderly goodnight. Again, those all-knowing eyes unnerved me.

I remembered Dick in the bathroom.

'Oh no! Oh Dick . . . what have you done?' I whipped the spastic boy quickly off his perch on the edge of the bath. He had been busy in my absence. He giggled at his handiwork. Brown lumps of shit smeared the walls. The mat and floor were soaked.

One hour later, I finished the floor and began to wash down the walls. Tears of frustration edged down my cheeks. I brushed them away. I had no time. Sal, the night nurse, arrived to find me shovelling the last of the shit into a bucket.

'Oh Lord! I can tell what kind of a day you've had!'

I couldn't speak. I couldn't stay. I washed quickly and disappeared into the night. The last bus was waiting to carry me home.

Over the next few weeks, I became a shadow of my former self. I ate, slept, and worked, kept my emotions on a tight rein. Bill believed he had beaten me into submission. He was boss. I played my role of wife dutifully and things cooled down for a bit. I suppose I needed something to rock me back on my heels.

23 September 1974
I returned home late after a particularly gruelling day at the Home.

Never off my feet since seven in the morning, my head hurt, my feet throbbed. Longing to sit down, I trudged up the stairs. The flat was in darkness. No sign of life. I fumbled with the key, and opened the door.

Black smoke billowed into my face. The acrid stench stung my eyes. Within seconds, tears were streaming down my cheeks. I felt for the light switch, and flung open the front door wide. I waded through the smog to the windows. In the kitchen, a blackened chip pan stood on its side. Hot fat had oozed off the draining board and congealed in the sink. On the cooker, a burner still glowed hot.

I gave myself no time to think. I raced downstairs to the couple on the ground-floor. Yes, they knew what had happened. Bill had been down earlier, pale and shocked, livid that his moustache had been set smouldering. They had given him a cup of hot, sweet tea, and he had gone off to work.

I went out into the street, glad of the cool fresh air on my face. In the nearest telephone kiosk, I dialled the factory number. Several extensions later I was connected with his boss.

'Is this an emergency?'

I explained the situation, and let him judge for himself. He seemed to agree.

'I'll have him sent home directly, in a company car. He should be about half an hour.'

He rang off abruptly.

Bill arrived home as promised, in a company car. As soon as he set foot in the flat, he started.

'What the hell did you do that for? I could have done without the lecture from the boss after you tittle-tattled to him. I'll be the laughing stock tomorrow.'

The smoke had cleared at last. The walls of every room bar the bedroom were coated with black dust. The floors were filthy, the furniture full of soot. He beat me up there and then in the hall. I let it happen. I had known it would come.

I toppled backwards as he pushed me towards the wall. My head cracked hard on the skirting board. I brought my hands up instinctively to protect my face. Like a fencing partner, he aimed his foot at the undefended parts. Wham! One in the stomach.

Crunch! One on the knee. Anywhere where it wouldn't show. My arms were pinioned to my sides as he brought his body down on mine.

'You slut!'

He slapped my cheeks hard. They began to burn. He released my hands. I moved them up to my face. But I had neglected to guard my bottom half. I felt my pants being pulled off me and fought him off with my feet.

'Bill. Not here . . . not now.'

'I'll show you, you cow. You'll do as I say.' I wished I had said nothing. I had only made things worse.

He shoved himself forcefully into position. In, out, in, out. The rhythmic heaving, the pressure on my body jarred on my nerves. My bruised back ached. My arms felt numb. But I had promised to love, honour, comfort and keep him, in sickness and in health.

24 September 1974

By 5 a.m. I had washed the walls and brought some semblance of order to the place. Even then the acrid smell still lingered. He sat smoking, watching and dozing in fits and starts. At six, he demanded breakfast. At seven, he went to bed. At eight, I left for work.

December 1974

The approach of Christmas. A time for caring, sharing, love. At the Home I spent my days dressing presents in pretty paper and ribbon. At night I returned home to a lonely, empty flat. Bill was always out. Out with the boys? His friends? Drinking? I didn't know. I didn't care. Just as long as he left me alone.

The blare of the stereo from below blotted out thought. Busy hands baking puddings, pies and cake prevented me sitting down to cry.

Carollers sang at the door, 'Be of good cheer . . . ring out the old, ring in the new.'

I'd had so many dreams for this, our first Christmas together. Where was the laughter, the love?

I blew my last fiver on a tree and decorated it with kitchen foil and cut-out paper fairies. It brought back a little of the magic that was missing, some of the sparkle I remembered from childhood. On the spur of the moment I decided to have a party—Christmas Eve it would be, to see the big day in. My larder was full of festive fare. Bill would provide the drink, I knew—I need have no worries on that score.

Christmas Eve 1974

The night of the party our little flat was full to overflowing. They were mostly Bill's mates with their girlfriends, but I didn't mind.

'Have some more trifle. Another piece of cake anyone?' I pressed.

'Swell food, Jan. Great party.'

The drink flowed early and freely as always. By nine it was running out.

'I'll go and get some more. Coming Dave?' said Bill. The two of them rolled drunkenly towards the door.

Suddenly, my smile began to wane. I was tired of the clamour, the confusion, the noise. Once again I was the proverbial wall-flower, enjoying it only through others. Now I was too tired to act a role any more. I wished they would all go. I sat in a corner and cried quietly inside.

'Come and dance, Jan.' It was Johnny. I had known him since the day he was best man at our wedding. He was a frequent visitor to our flat. I liked him. He seemed a decent guy. I smiled and turned away. He sat down beside me, and started to talk, nothing special, just whatever seemed to come into his head. I found myself listening despite my hurt inside.

'Hey, Chris, put something soft and sexy on the stereo,' he called. He pulled me up and put an arm gently around my waist. He couldn't have known what it did to me inside. It was a long, long time since a man had done that.

'I . . . I can't really dance. I mean, it's all this jigging up and down that gets me.' I hated to admit my inadequacy. My face turned red as I tried to make a joke of it. I moved back towards my chair.

'Come on, I'll show you.' His voice was soft, soothing, gentle. I responded, and we waltzed awkwardly around the floor.

'That's it, you're doing fine,' he encouraged. He made me want to do it well, to please him. Someone refilled my glass. I felt good, light-headed—happy? His arm still held me. I didn't want it to go, him to go. I wished the evening could last forever.

'Hi, we're back. Did anyone mizz me while I waz gone?' Bill's slurred voice jerked us apart. The party split up soon after that. People went home to bed. The last bus had gone long since, so Johnny was staying over. Still on an all-time high, I twirled in to thank him for the evening. Risking betraying my feelings, I teased, 'Come along now, time all children were tucked up in bed. Mummy's going to give you a goodnight kiss.'

I bent to kiss him lightly on the cheek. Instead he jerked me down to kiss me full on the lips. My emotions somersaulted and I pulled sharply away.

'What . . . what did you do that for?' I stammered, surprised at how my heart was reacting.

Tender fingers touched my cheek. 'Don't you know how I feel about you? I'd have had you myself if I'd only got there sooner.'

I ran out, back to my own bedroom—back to Bill, already asleep, and snoring heavily. I sneaked beneath the covers and dreamed of how things could have been.

Christmas Day 1974
Johnny made me a present of a woolly hat before he left in the morning.

'And I'll be calling often to see that you're wearing it . . .' were his parting words.

I smiled, and shut the door. I was still a part of yesterday—still living out the party, the goodnight kiss, and my somersaulting emotions. Maybe a glimmer of light was beginning to show at the end of the long, dark tunnel?

1975

Why is it harder to leave a loveless marriage than a loving one?
Because a loveless marriage is born of desperation, while a loving one is
born of choice.

ERICA JONG

New Year Day 1975
This year, I want to stand up for myself—I won't let him get me
down.

I want to make something of myself, my music.

I want to make my marriage work.

I want to somehow fulfil myself as a woman. To find that having
sex is exciting. Everything that it promises to be in books.

I want to have a child.

19 January 1975
Our first wedding anniversary.

We lay in bed. I was tense, nervous, crying. Bill raved on, 'Why
can't you be like other women? Look at yourself girl, you're a mess.
Ugly, frigid, frightened—what a combination!'

He stretched out his long, lithe, naked body as if he were God's
gift to women. I admired the ease with which he moved. He was
frightened of no-one.

'A man needs a woman to look after him. Cook and clean for
him. Make love to him. It's a fact of life. Didn't Mummy ever tell
you? But what have you ever done for me, except nag? When have
you ever satisfied my needs?'

I knew he was goading, taunting, plaguing me. I wouldn't rise to the bait. Wouldn't give him the excuse he needed to lash out. To inflict more violence. I'd play it his way.

Bill started to make advances. I froze. I was frightened. I couldn't cope. I didn't know any more how I felt or should feel. I only knew it would hurt. I couldn't understand my emotions. With Mum and Dad I felt swamped by their kisses. Yet there was nothing I wanted more at this moment than to be loved. To be shown that he loved me.

'There's only one way to take it. I don't like to hurt you, but . . .'

Afterwards, I cried myself to sleep in the spare room. I felt sick. Choked. Ashamed. I wouldn't even look at myself. I had been used. My feelings didn't matter. I didn't matter.

February 1975

My body was bruised and scratched—of my own volition! I had made every mark myself. It was an unexpected turn of events. Now I slammed out of the room during an argument, and listened behind closed doors, while Bill quietly and viciously swore, telling the air what he really thought of me.

'Rotten bleedin' cow! I'd like to break her bloody neck in two. Bitch! All I want is some fucking money.'

I'd go away to take out my anger on myself: scratching, clawing, hitting my head hard against the nearest wall. I couldn't do it all to him. I would only end up getting hurt far worse than he. So I did it to myself. I hated him for forcing me to this. I hated myself for allowing it to happen. Worst of all I hated me.

I hadn't planned it this way, it had just happened. Yet strangely, it was Bill who found it hard to accept. He hated the idea of his not having made the marks himself. At one point, he became distraught, 'Please Jan, please don't do this to yourself. Your scarred body looks so ugly.'

But somehow he didn't see it as ugly if his own marks were on it.

'Any man can beat his wife. It's part of being a man. If a woman can't accept who's boss then she just has to learn the hard way.'

'But Bill . . .'

'Oh shut up! Get on with my dinner and stop your blathering.'

43

I started to turn mirrors to the wall. He had told me so often I was ugly, I accepted it as fact. I was ashamed of myself, most of all for not being able to make this marriage work.

I looked to Mum and Dad. Their marriage worked. He didn't beat her. They could talk like adults without one or other of them getting so riled it ended up in a fight. They had arguments. Yes. But then so did any couple. What mattered was how each learned something from the other. They fitted together somehow, like two halves of a whole.

I wanted to be cuddled, kissed, made a fuss of, bought a box of chocolates or flowers every once in a while, without it having to be some kind of reward for being a good girl. What was the matter with me? Why couldn't I accept things as they were, instead of always wanting change? Perhaps then things would settle down. My hair was turning grey. My hands trembled most of the time.

Bill arrived home with his own guitar. He had always envied me mine. He twanged, and twiddled the knobs, breaking a string or two. Took money from my purse to buy more. The following week, he brought some friends round to the flat. Johnny was amongst them.

'Hi Jan, still wearing the hat? We're going into the Big Time, the rock music business.'

Every evening after that became an all-night sitting. They bought more and more equipment on HP. Speakers, amplifiers and mikes added to the long list of unpaid bills. The volume was turned up full. White noise blasted through the building on to the street below. It was deafening, demanded your full attention, distorted.

At the end of the month Hot Ayr had their first gig at the Carousel club. Luckily, I was working. I couldn't believe people would like them, and I returned home late that evening expecting all four to be drowning their sorrows.

They were drunk—but happy drunk—celebrating a resounding success. They had two bookings for the next month, and they were actually being paid. Fifteen pounds per gig. They had to have a whole new wardrobe. This meant more bills. Work was abandoned temporarily—at least by Bill—with the excuse he had to practise.

And I was jealous. Of course I was jealous. I had the qualifications, the know-how. Now, here was he, a beginner, having all the success. It made we want to give up.

3 March 1975

On my way to do an all-day stint at the Children's Home. I was late. Bill had needed money. I had none to give. He didn't believe me and grabbed my purse. He thought it was some trick to mislead him when he found it empty save for a few coppers. He took them anyway. Then, desperate for a fag, he made me help him carry out a fruitless search of the flat. My Post Office and bank books both proved penniless and he was forced to rummage in the waste bin for butts. This did not please him, but I was finally allowed to leave with only a hefty push to send me on my way. I hurried off along the street.

Suddenly, I found myself sprawled on the pavement. I didn't remember falling, but decided I must have tripped. It wasn't the first time it had happened. The previous week I'd fallen and gashed my leg, and laddered my tights. It was as if I'd blacked out. I'd had to ring work to tell them I wasn't coming, and, dazedly had made my way back home. I couldn't afford for that to happen again. I had to be more careful.

'Are you all right, my dear?' A lady took my arm, and pulled me back on the pavement. Somehow I had strayed on to the road in the path of oncoming traffic. My body shook. My legs had turned to jelly. I felt sick.

'I wasn't thinking. I'm all right, thank you. Really I am.'

Somehow, I dragged myself to the Home.

The Supervisor was kind. I was crying, living on the edge of my nerves. My hands wouldn't keep still as I sobbed out some of my troubles, jumping from one thought to another without any thread. She listened, then lent me fifty pence to get to the doctor's for a check-up. My mind kept fastening on the fact that I had a ten 'til eight shift to do. But she wouldn't let me. Instead, she saw me on to a bus.

'And don't come in tomorrow. Take the day off.'

I couldn't afford to, and knew I would be there.

The doctor seemed remote. He fiddled with his pad, played with his prescriptions, tapped a pen on the desk. It was distracting.

'You know, young lady, you can't expect to get married and live happily ever after. That only happens in fairy stories. Everyone has problems, marital ups and downs, little tiffs. You come to expect it.' He expounded his theories on marriage.

I felt a fraud.

'However,' he went on, 'you do seem to have got yourself in rather a state, don't you? If you're not careful you'll be having a nervous breakdown. It has come to the point in fact, when you have to choose—on the one hand, you have your husband and home, and on the other your work. It is up to you of course, but I would concentrate on your home life and on starting a family. For now, I'll give you some sleeping tablets and anti-depressants. That should help in the meantime.'

His words gave me a lot to think about. A child might solve things. Give Bill the incentive he needed to be kind, loving, caring. Make him take on his responsibilities as a father and husband. It might also work the other way. I wondered if he might try to harm the child, getting at me through it. Or if I wasn't around, take it out on our little girl or little boy. I was only too well aware from my work at the Children's Home how that child could end up.

I gave in my resignation at work. It was a gamble, a risk. I knew that from then on I would be even more dependent on Bill. It was hard saying goodbye to the children. It increased my ache inside for one of my own.

20 March 1975

'It's great having the little woman at home,' Bill boasted to his friends. 'It means I have a meal waiting on the table every day when I come in from work, and all that home cooking . . .'

I began to believe I had made the right choice.

More happiness—we were offered a maisonette. We had hoped for a house, but the Council's official word on that was: 'You must have two children, or else, after you have lived here a year, you may find an exchange you like. Let us know either way, and we will arrange it when the time comes.'

I was certain this would be the making of us. A maisonette in a new housing estate the other side of town. We could get away from this area altogether. Make new friends. A new beginning. Our chance to live in my dreamworld.

April 1975
The days are passing so slowly. Each one feels like a year. I feel so old—so much more than my 22 years. Life has no meaning for me any more, no reason, no purpose. I just want to curl up and die.

I stayed in bed until midday, didn't bother to dress. What was the point? Nobody cared if I lived or died. I'd done with trying to keep myself tidy—or the house, for that matter.

Last week I made a real effort. Spring-cleaned the house and had a dinner waiting for the worker just as it always was when he came home. But Bill didn't feel like mince, potatoes, and peas. He threw it across the room, splattering the wall and messing the carpet. The chip shop provided for his needs. Afterwards he fell asleep in the chair.

As for myself, I felt so ashamed. He asked me at every opportunity why I couldn't look like other girls.

'. . . big boobs, that's what I like,' he'd tell me. 'Big boobs, cheeky bums, and shapely waist and legs.' And 'Have you ever thought of having long, blonde hair?'

I ate 'comfort food' at night; bars of chocolate, a mug of sweet cocoa to go to bed on. It took my mind off the tomorrow looming up around the corner.

My depression became a living death, a living hell, and just when I thought I had reached rock bottom, then I'd fall another few feet. It was a quagmire dragging me down. It seemed to eat away at my very soul, leaving me an empty shell. I didn't walk, I shuffled. My body felt like lead. Everything was such an effort. My doctor kept me dosed with anti-depressants. They stopped me thinking, stopped me feeling, stopped me hurting inside, stopped me.

A woman across the way tried to commit suicide. Slashed her wrists. It was that kind of area. Three children, and a husband in prison. They took her away in an ambulance. I never saw her again. I began to think maybe that was a way out. Only I would use pills. Did I have enough? The idea took root in my mind.

2 May 1975

I counted my tablets. Spread them out over the table. A bottle of cider at my side—just in case! I didn't plan it in advance. I didn't sit down and say to myself, 'Tonight, I shall commit suicide. Tomorrow, I won't be here.'

I was in a drugged, confused state. The pills I was taking had that effect on me. They were powerful enough to fog my mind. I was lonely. I hadn't seen a soul in a week. I hadn't been out, and I had refused to open the door to visitors. I didn't want anyone to see me. Bill passed me by as if I were his shadow, and only spoke if he needed something. We lived like strangers.

I'd thought more than once about leaving. But to go back to my parents, admit I was wrong, was more than I could bear. Rather this than that. I didn't want to hear them say, 'I told you so.' Besides, I'd almost kidded myself into believing this way of life was the norm. Until now I had clung on to the hope that one day Bill would walk through the door a changed man—that he would treat me like a lady.

Persistent knocking brought me out of my trance. My fingers still clutched a handful of pills as I answered the door. I felt as if I were living a dream, seeing Johnny as if from a long way off. Suddenly, I broke down. I cried as if my heart would break. I had been on the edge for a long time, now I was falling over. The look of kindness, the gentle arm around my shoulder, the understanding word, had released my inner anguish. He made me sweet tea, and watched while I drank it. I felt all kinds of a fool, and realising what I must look like, covered my face with my hands.

'Don't look at me, I'm ugly,' I cried. But I didn't really want him to go.

'Oh, why amn't I a real woman? Why can't I be wanted, needed, loved as a woman should be? What's wrong with me?'

I reached for the pills.

But the time for that had passed. We mounted the stairs, and were standing in the bedroom.

'Come here,' a soft voice coaxed. 'I'll show you you're a real woman. Make you feel alive again.'

I walked towards the bed. Then, in a flash, saw Bill lying there, not Johnny.

'No!' I screamed.

'No! Not that!'

A hand held mine. We changed rooms, and moments later were together on the spare bed.

'It will hurt, you'll hurt me, and I'm sore,' I whispered. He took my clothes from me gently.

I felt awkward. My body shook uncontrollably. My eyes refused to focus. His hands were gentle, not hard and dirty like Bill's. He didn't want it for himself. He wanted it for me. I wasn't in love with him, I knew that. But it didn't hurt, and it made me feel a woman for maybe the first time in my life.

He dressed quickly, and left taking the pills with him. I lay for a long time, trying to come to terms with this new awareness. When I did move, it was as if I now had some purpose in life. My step had a new spring in it. I left Bill's dinner undone. I'd concentrate on my own needs for a change.

9 May 1975

I washed my hair, had it cut and styled, bought new clothes with money put by to pay the electric bill. Bill could worry for a change about what to do when the red letter came. I went out into the world, hesitantly at first. Then forced the pace a little so that I walked in the sunshine not in shadow. Made myself live by new rules, formed a new day by day plan to beat depression.

The next few months passed in what now represented normality in our marriage.

A CRYING GAME

Christmas Eve 1975

Alone, part of the party, yet apart. A glass of cider held in clammy hands, I tried to blend into the background. The music became a roaring in my ears. I felt as if I might faint. A fur coat brushed past me. A face peered into mine. The mouth was moving. Someone was speaking to me, but I couldn't hear. I smiled back, and turned away. A stabbing pain started up behind my eyes. I stifled a yawn. Almost midnight. When could we go home?

The music stopped. It was as if I had suddenly gone deaf. People held their breath, waiting for the magic moment to arrive. Outside, bells began to peal. A shout went up. Everyone was kissing and hugging everyone else. I had never felt so alone in my life. Like an onlooker. Near the stage I saw Bill in the arms of a slim blonde.

He left her to take up his position again on the platform with the band. Hot Ayr announced the finale. Johnny caught my eye, and smiled sadly. I heard the song being dedicated to me. Bill scowled. Then everyone took their partners for a final waltz. The opening bars of *Bridge Over Troubled Water* were just beginning as I slipped out of the door of the Club to fresh, clean air outside. Snow was falling. It was Christmas.

1976

The whole education of women ought to be relative to men. To please them, to be useful to them, to make themselves loved and honoured by them, to educate them when young, to care for them when grown, to counsel them and to console them . . . these are the duties of women at all times, and what should be taught them from their infancy.

JEAN JACQUES ROUSSEAU

19 January 1976
Our second wedding anniversary. Not even chocolates this time. He just didn't remember. I was drifting backwards into a depression. Already my resolutions were part of the past. We were rowing over little things now, like Bill forgetting to get bread and cheese when he went out to buy a new guitar; or the fact that I hadn't made my last pound stretch to something special for tea.

23 January 1976
Bill returned home at 1.30 a.m. Whereabouts unknown. He went out early evening, not saying where he was going.

27 January 1976
Bill didn't go to work.

28 January 1976
Bill didn't go to work.

30 January 1976
Bill didn't go to work.

2 February 1976
I was fed up with having electric guitars blaring until the early hours of the morning. I found myself a part-time job as a doctor's receptionist. It lasted exactly one month. I loved the work. Even the filing I did with enthusiasm and zest. The people were patient while I was learning, then later complained about the odour I had. I didn't understand it myself. All I knew was that if I panicked or was put under pressure, there was this smell. It was embarrassing. This lingering smell wafted around me, set me apart, made me different. It had lost me two jobs already—a part-time job in a shop and a four-day stint in a cash and carry. Now it was losing me a third.

My new employer, the doctor, would understand, I thought. I explained how it happened only when I was nervous, on edge, or excited. He prescribed tablets to take. Amplex tablets, two a day— for the rest of my life? Then he asked me to leave. I added the pills to my collection, and planned my next move.

11 February 1976
Doctor's appointment. I decided to discuss my being asked to leave my receptionist job with him. However, he had a discussion of his own that he wanted to pursue. Instead of the usual prescription for anti-depressants, he began asking questions. Personal questions.

'I've been meaning to ask you for some time, is everything all right at home—between you and your husband, I mean?'

'Yes, yes of course. Why?'

I couldn't tell him about my own private hell. At that time I wouldn't even admit to myself that I was being beaten. I was too close to the problem, and I refused to let go.

'There is one thing, though . . .' I added hesitantly. 'Is there anything wrong with me? When Bill comes near me I freeze. I find it difficult to communicate, to come together. He thinks I deliberately block his advances. I don't. It just hurts.'

There was an awkward silence. I shuffled uncomfortably in my chair. I began to wish I hadn't asked. But I wanted to know, so badly. I had to know if it was really my fault. The worry about being frigid, not having children, being afraid of sex, was eating me up inside. Besides, sex was becoming a central issue, a big bone of contention between Bill and myself.

The previous week we tried to make love. Bill was sober for a change and I was determined inside myself to succeed. I forced myself on through the inhibiting act of undressing, cowering down at the side of the bed to slip shyly out of my clothes. Then the painful point of penetration—I suddenly seemed to dry up. I was left lying naked, screaming with hurt. The more he forced, the more I tensed, panicked, cried, and screamed.

'I'm trying, really I am Bill. It just won't go.'

Bill didn't believe in foreplay. He barged straight in as usual and as always, came up against a physical barrier preventing entry.

'Open up, you little bitch.' A slap sent my head jolting to one side. He seemed to think I was doing this on purpose.

'Spread! Come on . . . spread those legs.'

I'd known then how this session would end—and I was right. He forced my legs apart. The watch on his wrist left a long red scratch on my flesh. It felt sore. My hand came away from my face with blood on it. I had bitten my lip.

Bed-clothes were snatched from the bed. The centre of the action changed to the floor. It was hard. My back hurt. He took hold of my breasts, pushing them round and round in a rough kind of caress. His nails dug in. He didn't seem to notice. He didn't seem to care. All he wanted was sex. Any way he could.

'Come on, you little bugger. Get in.' He was breathing heavily.

'Please Bill. Can we stop now?'

'Stop? We've hardly bloody started.'

'But Bill . . . it just won't go in.'

He pushed harder. He left my breasts and moved his hands down to my sides. They clamped down on one of my bruises. I leapt at least two inches into the air, screaming. Still he kept ramming, ramming, ramming. He was like a man deranged.

'I'm sorry, I'm sorry,' I sobbed.

I was always saying sorry, taking aboard the guilt. He threw me with force against the wall, and walked out. Didn't come home until the following morning. Didn't say where he'd been. My punishment was only ten pounds housekeeping. My dilemma was which of the seven outstanding bills, fines, and HPs to pay a little towards, which to leave.

The doctor was speaking again, gathering instruments together, pointing to the couch.

'Oh, you don't have to do anything. I just want your advice.' I wasn't sure what he intended, but I had a suspicion it would hurt. I still felt very sore, and I didn't want him to see any bruises that might remain. But he insisted.

'I promise I'll be very gentle.'

I'd never had an internal. It wasn't pleasant. I kept jumping, tensing at the wrong moment, moving involuntarily so that the whole thing took a lot longer than it should. Then I heard him catch his breath. I looked quickly away, feeling my face flush hotly. I thought he'd found a mark.

'But my dear, you're a mass of infection. No wonder it hurts!'

He prescribed me pills, more pills, different pills. As well as infection, I had a condition known as Vaginismus. It meant my vaginal muscles tensed involuntarily, closing together to become an impenetrable wall. It meant, even if I wasn't ready to reject Bill, my body certainly was. The doctor lent me a book on the subject, and I left with it importantly under my arm. I was seething. I was angry. I was mad. I meant to hit Bill between the eyes with this. I had other tests I must undergo, and it was plain that I was the wronged party in all this. I spent the bus ride home piecing together what I would say.

It never got said. Bill was in a foul temper. He had a lot on his mind—a finance company was threatening to take him to court. He was debating doing his usual trick if all else failed, of borrowing a hundred from another source to pay back this one. I kept my thoughts to myself and prepared a meal.

It was raining, so he wouldn't be going to work. Not even my new ploy of putting joke items in his packed lunch to coax him to go to work like a child to school, would make him change his mind.

It had worked at first. Liquorice, kid's sweets, rubber pencils, imitation pencils had enticed him to the factory. He had seemed to look forward to what he would find. It was a game that appealed to his sense of humour.

Everything he did seemed to be a game. A boy's game. As if he still had to learn how to grow up. Now he had his toy soldiers spread out over the floor. He was staging a mock battle and refused to be interrupted. It could go on for hours. I kept his dinner warm and ate mine alone in the kitchen. His would probably still be there tomorrow. We were on short rations that week and he hated making do.

'Why don't we ever have steaks?' he'd ask.

'How can we on the money you give me?' I'd retort.

'Well, other women get the same as you, and don't complain. Twenty-seven quid is a lot of money.'

I'd sigh heavily, know we were heading for an argument. I'd repeat the old refrain: 'But they probably don't have court fines to find, HP payments, finance loans, on top of the gas and electric and rent.'

27 February 1976
Bill brought home only £17 wages for the week.

12 March 1976
Bill bought new bass guitar.

20 March 1976
The doctor kept in touch. He wanted to see Bill on his own, probably to teach him about the finer points of passion. But Bill wasn't playing ball.

'It's you there's something wrong with, not me . . . I always said it was you, and now I've been proved right as always.'

He considered himself blameless. He wouldn't listen when I tried to say a little of what was weighing heavily on my mind. How did I get the infection? What about foreplay? What about feelings? What about Love? Could he not be more understanding, gentle, considerate? The words were foreign to him. I was his property to do with as he pleased. He turned the stereo up to blasting point, and closed his ears to my words.

19 April 1976
First time of having sex since February.

26 April 1976
The supermarket was crowded. It took me an age to get there, and I wanted to get down my list as quickly as possible. It was hot, humid, stuffy. Arms brushed past me sticky with sweat. I needed a new pair of tights. Mine looked old and laddered, and I was all too aware of my dowdy appearance. I wished I could do better. I stopped to envy a lady across the way who appeared fresh-faced, friendly, appealing.

The tins of peaches were on special offer. I put two in my basket, and crossed off the toilet rolls from my list. We could make do for another week. I headed for the till. There was a queue. My left leg hurt where my latest bruise was coming up a vivid shade of blue. I shifted uncomfortably from one foot to the other. Then the girl in front moved away, and I heaved my heavy basket up on to the rack. I wasted no time in putting the items into my bag, keeping a careful eye on the till roll to see I hadn't gone over my limit. A sigh of relief escaped me as the till totted up the amount.

'Six pounds eighty-seven pence, please.' The cashier looked harassed, impatient to see the end of the queue. The lady behind was already pushing to take my place. I reached into my purse. It was empty. I shook it, and it dropped to the floor.

'Come on, come on. I haven't got all day, you know!'
I stood still for a second, pale, dazed, shocked.

'Oh God, let me be wrong,' I prayed. It would be too, too embarrassing to have it happen to me. I picked up my purse, and looked again. Nothing. Not even an odd copper or two. I began taking the items back out of my bag, stammering apologies right, left, and centre.

'There's been some mistake,' I muttered.

'You bet there has.'

The cashier was furious. A supervisor was sent for, but the shop was just too busy to cope.

'I left my purse behind.' I was still trying to justify my situation.

'But you have it there, lady.'

'Oh, you just don't understand.' I was near to tears, and tried desperately to hold my emotions in check.

Customers behind wanted to get on. They began complaining about the delay, while I fiddled nervously with the edge of the tins. Still no supervisor.

'Look, I can't spend any more time on you. There are other customers waiting to be served,' the cashier began to scribble frantically on the till roll.

'What shall I do, then?' I enquired nervously.

'You'll have to put the things back in the basket, and go round the shop again to replace them, won't you?' She gave me a withering look, and I shrank to two inches high.

It took a long time, and those who hadn't heard what had gone before, looked at me a little oddly as I put the items back on the shelves. I dithered with the packet of tights. I felt even worse than I had when I first walked into the shop. I knew I wouldn't come back here in a hurry. A pair of eyes watched me from the next aisle—a store detective? It wouldn't have surprised me. I thought I looked suspicious. I replaced the last packet, and hurried out of the store.

'. . . but how could you do that to me? It was so embarrassing,' I raved at Bill later.

He shrugged, and turned the volume of the stereo up full. An easy way out when he didn't want to hear.

'What did you do with my money?' I had to shout to make myself heard.

'Your money? Who earns it? Who works his butt off for it? How can you call it *your* money. You're lucky to get any.' He slammed off the stereo, and stormed out. Moments later, I heard his latest possession judder into life, and jerk unsteadily off down the road.

The green van needed an MOT. Bill had only an out-of-date provisional licence from his motorcycle days. He didn't have insurance or tax. I knew if he got caught, I would have to bear the brunt.

May 1976
Sex and the lack of it apparently the reason for so many other complaints. Aloupecia for Bill and moods flaring up. Tension, especially at time of the month, for me. Frustration. I'm told it will be easier after we have a child—still no reason for having one. Love?

I embarked on a different course of action. Employers and employment bureaux weren't interested in giving me work as soon as they saw how tense and shaky I was. So I tried to get every smallest part-time job I could get my hands on: four hot, sweaty days in a fish and chip shop; selling Avon cosmetics to people in the flats round about—a foot-slogging, wearisome business; guitar tuition to four young pupils, an hour each week, at one pound a head. Anything that would raise a few pounds. I tried to make myself believe I was saving funds to leave him, to make a go of it on my own.

Jean Rich, my friend from next door, had just had a baby boy, and had also started work as a barmaid. She paid me half her wages to look after the child while she was working. She had her problems too—her husband went off with other women—and we'd often sit and share our troubles over a coffee at her place.

I answered an advert in the local paper for home envelope-addressing, and received by return of post a list of firms who would be interested in my services. I started at the top and worked down. But all that was sent after six weeks of waiting was a parcel containing one thousand yellow leaflets for distribution. One thousand! It seemed I had to post these through allotted doors—for which there would be no payment. Only then could I move on to 'bigger and better employment'. The accompanying letter called it a kind of initial test to replace the usual interview. When my worthiness and dedication had been proved, I would be sent details of how to begin my envelope-addressing in earnest.

It didn't make much sense to me. I spent a couple of weeks trying to locate the elusive company concerned, then I ditched the leaflets in the bin.

While I continued to answer adverts for childminders, and contact Social Services about home-help work, Bill and I led separate lives. Weekends I spent alone. Weekdays I worked at making the budget eke out. And I ate. I ate as a substitute for love, and now, when he stole five pounds from my purse, he fobbed me off with apologies of a late-night Chinese take-away, or chocolates. It was a beginning, but it made me feel I was being bought. I ate them anyway.

Bill thought the extra money I was bringing in entitled him to help himself. We didn't talk to one another any more. My words, my voice, Me irritated him, and I remained out of his way as much as possible. He preferred the company of Hot Ayr and the ceaseless round of records, booze, and fags.

7 June 1976
Bill didn't go to work.

10 June 1976
Bill spent £30 wages. I don't know what on.

12 June 1976
Discovered he was behind on HPs. Court action threatened.

17 June 1976
Bill didn't go to work. Because it was raining!

19 June 1976
In arrears with rent as well as HP.

27 June 1976
It was a stormy night. Our rowing continued until the early hours.

'This is it, Bill. I'm leaving. I've had enough.' I'd said the same thing so often as a threat, he just didn't believe me any more. I hardly believed I ever would myself. It had become something to say.

'OK. I'll help you pack.' He grabbed a suitcase from the top of the wardrobe and began to fill it with clothes. It stunned me for a moment. He really meant it.

Bill retired to bed at that point, assuming I'd be gone when he woke. I stared down at the suitcase for a long, long time. I took it downstairs, and left the house. Then I caught the early-morning bus for Birmingham.

My parents were staggered to see me arrive.

'Pet, what a wonderful surprise. Lovely to see you.'

I felt warm inside. Welcomed. Loved. They thought it was an ordinary visit, decided on the spur of the moment. They assumed I'd be staying for a few days.

I caught the next bus back home. My sisters had been having talks with our parents about their futures. I didn't want to be the black cloud on the horizon. Bill was asleep when I tiptoed back in and made tea. He had been asleep all day and was unaware that I had ever gone.

July 1976
His body bore down on mine. Pounding, pushing, pummelling, pinning me to the bed. He swore softly, crudely, and shifted position. I could feel bones through flesh. Long nails that needed cutting scratched my legs. Glazed eyes stared vacantly into mine. It wasn't me he was doing it with, but probably the girl of his dreams. I felt used, second-hand, cheap. He called it 'making love', but nothing could have been further from the truth. It was rape. Cold-blooded, calculated rape.

I hated myself for putting up with it, as fingers found a hold. I gasped at the onrush of pain. It came over me in waves. My mind screamed for a return to sanity. I became demented, deranged, temporarily mad. My body wriggled and writhed, crying out to be left alone. He held me fast. There was no mercy in him. He would get his due.

'Bill. Let me be. Let me go. Leave me in peace.' My words fell on deaf ears. If anything, the pace of progression slowed. Things were not going well, and this was always my dread. It only made the situation worse, and extended the whole proceedings. I tried to accept things as they were, to lie back and think of anything else but the here and now. It sometimes worked if I imagined my own dream man, but the beery breath and the bristles scratching my cheek, always brought me back with a vengeance to the present.

My left hand moved to the side to get a grip on the pillow. A pair of scissors that had been lying on the dressing table slipped to the floor. Bill's regular writhing movements never faltered once as I reached down after them. I clutched the cold steel. It gave me the courage to do what I had to do. Then, and only then, would I be free. Free from oppression, guilt, despair. Free to live, laugh, and love again.

I drove the points home with all the anger, the venom, the fury that was in me. A look of surprise etched itself across his face, before the pain began to take over. His body felt heavy, limp. I was shaking as if in shock, living again the memory of that fatal moment. Then I awoke—it was all just a bad, bad dream.

There was a footfall on the stair, a muttering and cursing. Then the bedroom door banged open.

'Hiya. How's about a bit of nooky?' It wasn't so much a question as a statement. My dream was about to become reality, at least in part. He had come to claim what he believed was his.

He stumbled into the room. Drunk. His hand jerked his belt undone, fumbled with his zip. It caught in his pants, and he pulled angrily to get them apart. There was a ripping sound. He stepped free of his clothes to bare his bony body. The bed creaked and groaned in protest. I tried to turn away, to be brave, to refuse to play ball. But it would only make things worse in the end.

He clawed at my nightdress. I saw he held a half-finished fag. A smouldering cigarette end can be lethal in the wrong hands. I knew to my cost. I had already had my hair singed while Bill had been in the act of teasing me with the lighted end. He liked to taunt me, holding me rigid as the end wafted near my nipples, my belly button, my vagina.

Now he launched himself into the attack, while I moved to my defence. I prayed it would not take long. My body, still sore with infection, ached for a reprieve. I wanted to scream and shout, to strike out at the enemy. Instead, I lay tense and still.

Bill's body pressed down on mine. I felt suffocated as if all the breath were being pushed out of my body. A pair of scissors lay on the dressing table. They tantalised me to the point of distraction as I remembered my dream. But they remained out of reach, and the rape continued.

He came to the point where he could go no further. The impenetrable wall shut him out as an alien. He lay back, breathless and spent. But the worst was still to come. He made me do things I didn't want to do. Things that sickened and repelled me. He made me kneel in front of his frustrated body. His hand held my hair tightly, painfully, pushing my face down into his hair. He pushed his penis into my mouth. I gagged. Vomit threatened. My stomach somersaulted. I wanted to be sick.

'Come on, you bitch. Make me come.'

The thought of it was enough. I pulled away sharply, leaving some of my hair in his hands. He grabbed my face, forcing my mouth to open. He jerked me down like before.

'Come on, come on, come on.' He pushed my head down and up, down and up, in time with his words. Suddenly his body went rigid. He pulled me up to his torso, gripped my hair savagely, and forced me to lick him from top to toe. Then it was over for another night, another week, maybe even a month.

Later that same day, we had to call in the police to report a burglary. The equipment belonging to Hot Ayr had been stored downstairs, and now we discovered Bill's amplifier was missing. It was strange that the thief had taken only that one item, when there was other much more expensive gear. The police thought so too. I said nothing. I was remembering that Bill was behind on the payments, and that he had received a letter from the company concerned, giving him seven days to pay, or else. The amp was never seen again.

11 August 1976
Bill refused my request for £10 more per month to pay bills and keep out of arrears.

17 August 1976
Beginning of weekly appointments with doctor. On tranquillisers due to strain at home and money worries.

31 August 1976
3 months behind with payments to tailor's.

September 1976
Another year of our marriage was dragging slowly to a close and still nothing had changed for the better. Bill seemed more than ever like a little boy, with his constant need for games, his mock battles with toy soldiers. At times it was as if he were trying to see how far he could push me. He stayed out late, came home drunk, and couldn't get up for work next morning.

He often brought home ten pounds or less as his wages, having spent most of it on sweets, fags, and booze. I was lucky if I saw a couple of pounds. Any bills or ominous red letters that arrived, he stashed away unopened in a drawer, as if they'd somehow go away of their own accord. And he was forever complaining about meals.

'Eggs again—but we've had them twice this week already!'

'And you've got them again tomorrow,' I'd retort. 'You're lucky to have a meal at all with the money you bring in.'

'You go out and get a job then. I feel shut in. An animal trapped in a cage. Marriage did that to me! Marriage—and you! You've chained me up like a prisoner, and I hate, hate, HATE IT!'

The bit about me getting a job struck in my craw. I was always answering adverts, then being turned down when I arrived for an interview. I couldn't keep from shaking. I couldn't hold a cup and saucer without using both hands. But from then on I was determined to show him.

When I arrived at the plush hotel I felt so dowdy. It didn't help when I was greeted by the glamorous girl behind the desk.

'Can I help you?' She looked as if she'd stepped off the front cover of *Vogue*. I wilted into the wallpaper.

'. . . I'm here for an interview,' I replied hesitantly. 'For the job of receptionist.'

She summed me up with a look.

'Sit over there, and you will be called, Mrs . . . Miss?'

'Mrs D_____, thank you.'

But instead of going to the chair, I moved towards the door. This place wasn't for me. I'd only bring down the tone of it. The girl called after me, and I broke into a run. I didn't stop running until I stepped on to the bus that would take me home.

I stayed a little longer at this next interview. It was another receptionist job, this time at a small surgery. I'd spent the money put by for the gas bill on a new twelve-pound coat. At least it hid whatever I wore underneath. I had a little more self-confidence as I entered the office, knowing I'd done this kind of work before.

'Could you do a specimen of your handwriting?' Pleasantries over, they moved quickly on to the business side of things. ' . . . And have you a reference? Why did you leave your last place of employment?'

My hand shook, and my writing took on a spidery appearance. Every word was an effort. Raised eyebrows, covered glances. How could I explain about the dreaded smell, the odour I was sure even now was making its presence felt? I was sweating. The office was stuffy. I wished I hadn't come.

'Well, thank you for coming, Mrs D_____. We'll be in touch if we need you.' With a word, a nod, and the official handshake, I was dismissed. They weren't even waiting for my explanations. They had already made up their minds.

Two or three times a week now I'd mention I was leaving, packing my bags and starting a life of my own. No-one believed me—least of all myself. I was still afraid of being alone, of having no-one to look after and come home to, I was frightened of having to think only of myself, and of giving up my home and husband. For what?

When it came down to it, I was scared. Too scared to go. Afraid to stay.

Encouraged by Jean Rich's husband, Jeff, I started jogging sessions at six in the morning. Running got rid of my rage. It left me so limp, so tired, I had no energy remaining to think or feel. Yet at the same time, I experienced exhilaration, excitement. I was aroused by it.

Together, we would slog slowly, tediously, exhaustedly around the park, and end up on a bench for a chat before crawling home. One morning, however, two policemen were there to meet me when I had circuited the field for the fourth wearisome time. A woman who lived in a house overlooking the park had telephoned them.

'Now then, Miss. You're quite safe now.'

'Quite safe?'

'Yes, we'll deal with him now.'

'Deal with who?'

Jeff arrived on the scene at that moment.

'OK. If you'd like to come along with us.'

'What is all this?' Jeff was indignant. I was too puffed to say or think anything. But the police were only too willing to explain.

'We received a phone call to the effect that there was a young man chasing a young lady through the trees in the park. We are here to offer assistance.'

It would have been funny if it hadn't been so serious.

Jeff was constantly offering to drive me away from Bill and the beatings, to my parents in Birmingham. He was concerned. He and Jean could hear our rows all too clearly through the wafer-thin walls of the maisonette. He and I on these morning runs would talk about what my life could be like, and for a short while after, I'd be happy with my dreams. Then reality would return.

I sang at Old-Age Pensioners' Clubs, schools, hospitals, churches. I wrote concerts on a theme about faith, hope, and love.

'Love between two people can be a very happy and wonderful thing,' I'd preach to my audiences, as if I had a wealth of experience behind me.

Afterwards, they'd shake me by the hand, thank me for coming, and say, 'You are obviously a lucky girl, and a very happy one. Very much in love with life, and your husband . . .'

I lived my dreams through the songs I sang, and it was almost a psychic shook afterwards, to be jolted back to the present.

September 1976

I returned home one evening just ahead of Bill, still euphoric. It had been one of my best concerts. I'd sung until my voice was hoarse, and we'd finished with a medley of the 1930s songs I loved so much.

Still singing *A Nightingale Sang in Berkeley Square*, I had just put on the kettle, when Bill rolled in. Where he had got the money to buy drink this early on, I had no idea. It was suspicious, but he was in no mood to be questioned. I thought I was used to seeing him drunk, but this was one of his worst times. He was all but paralytic, and just when I was at my happiest for months, I bumped back down to earth.

'Get outa my way, you bitch.' He pushed me roughly aside, and made for the sink. Missing his target, he was sick on the floor. Vomit clotted on the lino. My mood quickly changed from anger to disgust. It would be me who would have to clear it all up.

'Ah, that's berra!' He gave a long low burp. 'Now, gotta have a pee.'

I suddenly wondered what he had in mind. I had never seen him so drunk. I was scared.

The stairs bore the full flood of the waters.

'Bill . . .,' I screamed. 'Not there!'

'Where then, where then?' he asked, mimicking my tone. I tried to pull him up the stairs, over the puddles trickling down. It occurred to me how easy it would be to simply push him down the other way. To push him down the stairs and run. He evaded my grasp, and headed back into the kitchen.

'For heaven's sake, Bill . . .,' I agonised, seeing him reaching up to spill a stream of beery urine into the pans of veg and meat on the cooker. I felt sickened. Useless. I tried to pull him away, dragging at the trousers dangling around his knees. I wanted to take hold of his penis and yank. I knew it was the one place I could strike back. He would take it as a threat to his manhood. But I was sure if I did so he would kill me. He would have no way of stopping himself in the state he was in.

It was useless. I wasn't sure if he was deliberately egging me on, goading me in his usual way, or really was too drunk to know where the bathroom was. Then he started to climb the stairs, and teetered off balance halfway up. I pushed him the rest of the way from behind.

'Leave me alone,' he yelled. 'Leave me alone.' He shoved me heftily out of his way. I lost my footing, and fell back down into the hallway.

My head was swimming, my left arm hurt. A bump the size of a a golf ball was rising rapidly on my leg. Every part of me ached. I climbed up on to the landing with an effort. Bill was sprawled on the double bed. He'd passed out. A cigarette lay smouldering on the bedclothes. I picked it up, and threw it out of the window. I almost threw myself, I felt so wretched. Then I stepped gingerly down the stairs, gagging at the stink, and headed next door for sympathy. Jeff was livid. He wanted to punch Bill where it would hurt, but I wouldn't let him.

Next morning, Bill didn't remember a thing. He had a raging headache, and swore I was making the whole thing up just to get at him. I wished then I'd left the mess as it was. But I'd only have had to clear it up later.

Pregnancy test positive—I was ecstatic! I'd been putting on weight for weeks, despite all my jogging and dieting. My doctor had asked me to give in a sample at the Women's Hospital, and I'd done so with mixed feelings.

Despite my longing for a child, my hopes that a child would change Bill, when it became a possibility that a baby was on the way, I wasn't so sure it would solve anything. One question filled my mind: what if he hit the baby as well as me? My work at the Children's Home had taught me enough to be aware of the psychological effect caused by environment on a child. Other doubts nagged. If Bill continued as he was, we wouldn't have enough money to give the baby a proper home. How would we manage? I would never forgive him if our child was deprived.

My doubts lessened when I broke the news. He was delighted. Over the moon. He kissed and hugged me, and left for work singing.

'Oh Jan, you've made me so happy. You've made me so proud. You'll see, I'll make it all up to you.'

I wanted so much to believe this, but I was still unconvinced. I felt in my stomach that things would return to normal soon enough.

Yet somehow they changed. He changed. Over the next few weeks, he worked overtime to pay some of the outstanding bills. He even acquired a weekend job as barman at a pub down the road. I had his company in the evenings when he wasn't playing with Hot Ayr. He became so kind, so thoughtful and gentle, it was like having a new man. I wasn't allowed to carry cumbersome shopping bags, and every chore he did with a smile on his face. My hopes had been rewarded. My dearest dreams had come true.

18 October 1976
Bills now in arrears £58.62

4 November 1976
Car insurance in arrears and action threatened.

13 December 1976
Took £5 from my purse although he knew it wasn't my money, but for Avon orders.

22 December 1976
Found a payment card for a new guitar and case. I knew nothing about it.

1977

This is the true nature of home—it is the place of peace, the shelter, not only from all injury, but from all terror, doubt and division, a sacred place, a temple of the hearth.

JOHN RUSKIN

5 January 1977
Dear Mum and Dad,

It was lovely being with you all at Christmas and thank you for all you did to make it so happy.

I begin babysitting again this weekend for Jean and will be glad of my new hobby of knitting toys, especially if Bill decides to go out and I am on my own as usual. I too dream of what it would be like if we lived nearer, perhaps in the same street; and could share a cup of coffee and do our shopping together. In the lonely evenings, it would be particularly appreciable and we could take it in turns to keep one another company.

But these are just dreams and at least I have a new venture to occupy my time. It does seem rather appropriate at the beginning of a new year!

The months ahead will no doubt bring many changes, as well as good times and bad. However, with our preparations for our first child I now have things to plan for. I realise only too well it won't be a bed of roses and I shall get moody and depressed some days. Also, it is likely to prove difficult with Bill working nights, and having to cope on my own much of the time.

I have a positive ache for a baby to hold at times. I know I have enough love to offer him several times over. I just hope I can gather together some of the material things he will need over the next twelve months. Of course, there is also our holiday to Yarmouth with you that I am very much looking forward to and I need to save as much as I can towards it. Bill now has three part-time jobs—he had a lot of debts to pay. But don't worry . . .

We saw the New Year in at the Carousel Club singing Auld Lang Syne on stage with Hot Ayr. It was a moment to remember. Afterwards, everyone began kissing everyone else which went on for a good half hour. We eventually crawled into bed around three in the morning.

Come and have tea with us on our anniversary if you can. Make a day of it. It would be lovely to have someone to share it with.

Looking forward to seeing you soon,
Janine.

27 January 1977

My pregnancy—my phantom pregnancy—lasted just three months.

The doctor commiserated, 'If you want something badly enough, then sometimes you can begin to make it happen.'

All the signs, the symptoms were there. I was sick in the mornings. The sight and smell of tea and coffee repelled me. I grew in size, and could even boast a little lump. But there just wasn't anything there.

I felt so empty. My body ached for the child that wasn't to be. My whole being cried out with loss. Within the week Bill reverted back to his old ways. I was left alone once more with my dreams.

Loneliness is like a disease. It eats away at the human heart until there is nothing left. I hardly see Bill now. I am on edge, careful to keep out of his way, fearful of my every move, every word, lest it upsets him. Money, bills, the future, myself, are all taboo subjects. They irritate, antagonise, and lead to arguments which in turn end in beatings. It is as if the last few weeks never happened. Loneliness breeds discontentment. Discontentment breeds hate, and hate can destroy a person's will to live.

For three months, I'd been happy. Now, once more, all I had for company were broken promises and lies. We were living like strangers. Why did I stay to take more and more of this undeserved punishment? I stayed because I would not, I could not go. Something inside me—pride or foolishness—prevented me taking the final step.

5 February 1977

Doors banged. Chairs scraped. Voices chattered. Teacups clattered in saucers. People began to take their places.

'Can I have your attention, please . . .?'

The Over Sixties Club shuffled into their seats. The concert was about to begin.

'This afternoon, ladies and gentlemen, I have great pleasure in welcoming a very dear friend of ours. She needs no introduction I'm sure, and without more ado I shall pass the meeting over to Mrs D_____.'

I looked reprovingly in the speaker's direction. 'Janine, please,' I murmured as spontaneous clapping broke out.

My cheeks burned. My body sweated. The bruise on my leg began to throb. I fiddled with the music stand, shuffling papers to give my hands something to do.

'I'll wait until you're all quiet . . .' I began, struggling to secure the guitar strap.

'Shush, shush,' an agitated front row whispered around the hall.

'I'm very pleased to be with you all again,' my voice shook a little. My throat went dry. 'For those who don't know me, my name is Janine, and this afternoon I bring you my own brand of humour and music. Not pop. Not folk. But songs written by me especially for you.'

Stomach cramps began to ease. Fingers found the chord of E major. I strummed jauntily into the first song.

Love is everything that money cannot buy,
It begins with the simple things of life.
Love can make you sing, love can make bells ring,
Love is everything to me . . .

My voice rang with conviction. Faces beamed up at me. I smiled back. Confident. Sure.

'What are your favourite words? Can you tell me the words that you most like to hear?' I fixed a lady in the second row with a quizzical stare.

'Apple pie,' came an amused voice from the back. Laughter rippled around the hall. Others took the cue.

'Spotted Dick,' shouted another.

'Coronation Street,' added a third.

A couple near the back began a shaky, out of tune rendering of the theme music.

'No, no, no,' I sighed exaggeratedly, with a vigorous shake of the head.

'I love you,' I shouted, crisp and clear.

'We love you too,' came back the reply.

I launched into my next number, a wobbly smile on my lips. I felt choked. My leg hurt. My bruised thigh felt numb.

Love stands for care, and honesty,
All of the good things that we'd like to be.
Love is to be loved and loved in return—
Caring, sharing, trust and concern . . .

My breaths were almost sobs. I gulped air trying to regain composure.

'Now. . . what does the word 'Love' conjure up? Two people. Engagements. Flashing emeralds, perhaps?' If only, I thought. 'Candlelit dinners, holding hands, laughing, loving? But then look what happens? You get married and there are always dishes to wash, baths to clean, floors to scrub, dinner to do. Chores. Never-ending chores. What becomes of all those romantic ideas? Where do all those tender moments go? Down the plug hole along with the dirty bath water?' I tried to keep my voice light, bantering, kidding them along.

'Well my next song is dedicated to all you hard-working house-wives out there.'

Get back to the kitchen, Woman,
Get back where you belong.
It's not your place to play a guitar,
To write or sing a song.
You're just a woman—
One of the weaker sex—

Your place is the kitchen
To wipe and clear the mess.

Bill's words.

Woman, what are you doing?
I want my dinner soon.
Get on with the cooking,
Don't ask for the moon.
Woman, I don't want to know
About the price of food.
You're the one who buys it—
I'm not in the mood!

Everyone loved it. I could tell from their faces.

Pick up your dish mop, pick up your bowl,
Pick up your dishes too.
This is your place and you must keep pace,
I have to finish the Pools.
But don't get any ideas
About picking up a book.
Get back to the kitchen, Woman—
You've got my dinner to cook!

Thunderous applause. People laughing, clapping, standing in appreciation of a good song. I felt physically exhausted. Mentally drained. My head ached. My bruised leg throbbed. My mind was numb. This was my life I was singing about, my life they were applauding.

'Thank you, thank you, thank you everyone.'

Shakily, I walked to the side of the stage. I grasped a pile of tatty papers and returned to my place. Everyone was still. Quiet. Expectant.

'I was having a spring clean the other day. You know how it is. You wake up feeling that today is the day. It has to be today. Dusters, mop, polish, hoover all come out the cupboard. But then, right at the back, I came across these.'

I blew across the top of the pile, watching with satisfaction as a cloud of dust—flour?—flew up into the air. I blew again for effect. People laughed. I pulled at a sheet yellowed with age and carefully opened it out.

'*News of the World*', I read out slowly, 'April 28, 1940.'

A man on the front row gasped, moving forward in his seat. I had everyone's attention.

'Now then . . . let me see . . .' I rustled the papers and ran a finger along the columns headed: 'Missing from Home', 'Call for Women', and 'What War is Costing Us'.

'Ah, here it is. It says: "Whisky will be increasing to 16s a bottle, Gin to 15s 6d a bottle".'

The hall was so quiet I could hear the uncomfortable wheeze of the gentleman in the third row back.

'"Cigarettes will cost 8½d for 10 and to post a letter you will now have to pay 2½d . . ." Ah, those were the days.'

A murmur of agreement whispered along the rows of listeners. This was what they liked to hear.

'The following is a preciously preserved extract from a love-letter written to his wife at home by a soldier on active service: "Don't send me no more nagging letters, Letty. They don't do me no good. I'm many miles away from home, and I want to enjoy this war in peace".'

People clapped, talked, cried a little.

'And now, in the words of Semprini—some old ones, new ones, loved ones, neglected ones.' I seated myself at the piano with a flourish. An assortment of 1938 songs confronted me. I chose one at random and listened for the well-known tune to catch on. More followed. *A Nightingale Sang in Berkeley Square, Down at the Old Bull and Bush, Carolina Moon, If You Were the Only Girl in the World.* Tears flowed freely down my face. I wished this moment would never end. This was the real Me. Not the cowed, submissive slave I was at home with Bill.

'We must finish soon. It's almost four,' a voice whispered in my ear.

I brought the concert to a close.

We'll meet again
Don't know where, don't know when,
But I know we'll meet again
Some sunny day.

Strains of the old familiar melody seemed to go on and on forever. Clapping. Closing prayers. Scuffling of feet. Scraping of chairs.

'Mrs D_____. Janine?' A lady I remembered seeing somewhere in the sea of faces approached me. I turned to grasp her hand.

'I just wanted to thank you,' she said. 'To thank you for such a lovely afternoon. I loved that song: *Get Back to the Kitchen, Woman.* You must have a very happy life to write like that and be so in love with your husband. You're very lucky.'

I avoided her eyes. Pushed music into a bag. Stuffed guitar into a case.

'Anyway thank you.' She disappeared into the crowd. I grabbed my bits and pieces and left.

7 February 1977

My first really brutal attack, from which I sustained injuries. What had gone before seemed mild in comparison.

It was a cold, wet Monday, and Bill had been out with Hot Ayr. He returned for tea unexpectedly, complaining bitterly. I was washing dishes in the kitchen.

'What, no tea made for me?' he demanded.

'I wasn't expecting you. You didn't say what time you would be back.' I always seemed to be on the defensive, shouldering the guilt.

'And the gas has gone out. What did you let it go out for? Do I have to do everything around here?'

He bent down to light it, and I laid a warning hand on his arm. 'Bill, watch out for your cigarette.'

He shook his arm free. 'I know, I know. Do you think I'm stupid, or something? Get back to the sink, woman. Maybe you'll get around to making me something to eat eventually.' The sneer in his voice warned me that he was angling for an argument.

'Please Bill. I've just started a period, and I don't feel well. Leave me alone.'

It was like a red rag to a bull. The excuse he had been looking for. Maybe it was me not doing my wifely duties, or the whine that had entered my voice, or maybe he would have done it anyway. His right arm lashed out like a whip. I caught it full force on my cheek. It stung. I tasted blood. I felt sick. The sting stayed with me as I tried to leave the room. I wanted out. But he blocked the doorway with his frame.

'Stop acting like a swine, and let me go . . . now!'

His right arm moved like lightning. I felt rather than saw it hit my jaw. I heard a crack and bit my tongue. I had to massage my jaw back into place.

'Bill . . .' My tongue was like a blockage in my throat. 'Bill . . . Will you stop it?' I tried every tactic I knew. Appeal. Anger. Finally escape. But there was no place to run.

I saw the bread knife on the draining board. As a last desperate attempt to keep violence at bay I took hold of it. Threatened. Thrust menacingly at him each time he came near.

'Keep away, Bill. I warn you. I'll use it.' He backed off. I tried to edge around him out of the door. But he wasn't frightened enough to move away completely.

I saw him start towards me. I had to do something. I didn't have the courage to use the knife on him. He knew it. I turned the knife on myself. I closed my eyes for a split second, praying for the strength to do what I intended. When I opened them again, he looked like a snake ready to strike. I couldn't hold him off much longer.

I tried to plunge the knife into my belly. He uncoiled and sprang at me like a tiger from the corner of the room. All hell broke loose. I felt his fingers tightening around my neck. Squeezing. Suffocating. I dropped the knife with a clatter, cutting my hand on the blade. Blood oozed out. I could feel it, warm and sticky. A gash across my palm. I tried to keep my face covered as I hit the floor. The kitchen tiles came up to meet me. Then I must have passed out.

I came to in a rain of kicks. He kicked me and kicked me. Over and over again. Feet jabbing viciously in soft flesh. His face looked evil. Never had he looked so ugly, so menacing. This was my husband. The realisation hit me as if for the first time.

Pain didn't register at first. I felt numb, as if I were sitting on the edge of a precipice. I dragged myself up on to wobbly legs and headed for the door. It was far in the distance at the end of a long, dark tunnel. It seemed to take me an age to reach it. I dragged myself into the living room, and clung on to the sofa. Then he appeared from out of the mist fogging my brain and started on me again as if I were a punchbag. I put out one weak arm in an effort to fend him off. Then I collapsed.

I don't know how long I was unconscious. When I came to, I was heaped on the carpet at the back of the sofa. I peered around the edge. Bill was sitting with a bottle of beer and a bag of chips, watching a comedy show on TV. He looked relaxed, and was actually smiling. How could he smile after what had happened? My mind stalled. I slid back on to the floor and waited until he left for work. He didn't so much as look my way. He just banged out of the flat in his usual fashion. The slam of the door caused a thunderous roar to reverberate inside my head.

8 February 1977

His first words were, 'God, you look a mess.'

I didn't dare look in the mirror. It was enough to be told. Swollen bruises coloured my right side. My hip hurt when I walked. All I could see of my stomach were large black and blue blobs. Both shoulders ached from being slammed against the wall. My head hurt, and a blinding headache developed into migraine bringing spots before my eyes. As well as anti-depressants, I took two painkillers every four hours.

I slept in the spare room for a while after that, and refused to budge from the flat until my injuries had healed. I was embarrassed. Too much of a failure to consult a doctor for help.

13 February 1977

Took Avon money from my purse.

11 March 1977

A routine has now been established. Bill sleeps all day, getting up in time for a meal before going on nightshift. Practises with Hot Ayr every Saturday, then plays out on gigs with them until one or two the next morning. Spends Sundays at a friend's house working on the car.

28 April 1977
Bill took the night off work due to car running out of petrol. Still driving it with a provisional licence.

5 May 1977
Bill took night off work.

16 May 1977
Bill changed to a dayshift in an effort to leave me on my own less.

26 May 1977
Found that Bill had taken money from my purse. He had also spent the money Hot Ayr had given him to give to me. I was paying an HP for them by agreement.

1 June 1977
Bill spent group's money again instead of giving it to me to pay. Consequently now in arrears.

2 June 1977
Discovered he has taken my Avon money again and spent it. Was now having to hide Avon and catalogue money. Tried having sex for first time in several months.

20 June 1977
Bill took day off work to see about buying a new car.

21 June 1977
Bill off work again.

30 June 1977
Bill disappeared after tea not even saying where he was going. Arrived home after midnight. I spent the evening phoning round trying to locate him.

14 July 1977
Bill disappeared late afteroon. Arrived home after midnight.

23 July 1977
Holidays at last after months of worry and waiting. Pleased to be able to give my parents the promised holiday, I tried to put out of my mind the money it had meant borrowing from the bank. I couldn't put out of my mind though the large white Zephyr bought by Bill just before we went away. Bill had just driven home one morning in it instead of the green van—and said nothing.

'I haven't seen that car before around here, have you?' I commented at breakfast. I said it more to make some sort of conversation to break the strained silence, than out of any real interest.

'Yes, as a matter of fact, it's mine.' He carried on eating as if it were an everyday occurrence for him to buy a car.

'But how . . . I mean, where did the money come from?' I felt sick at heart, somehow dreading the answer.

'Money, money, money, that's all you think about. You tight-fisted bitch. We've got it, that's all.'

He stormed out up to bed, while I hurried to check the savings. They were all gone from their hiding place, every last penny. There had been almost two hundred pounds in cash for the holiday. Bank and Post Office Savings books had been too easy for him to check on. I'd known it was a stupid idea from the start to keep money in the house, but I was running short of ideas. Now we had nothing; only the money put by for bills, and my Avon collections.

'You fucking bastard,' I screamed. Tears streamed down my face. I was so angry, I thought I would burst with emotion. But it was wasted on him. He lay smoking in bed, a sardonic smile on his face. It only made me feel worse, but I was at a loss as to know how to hurt him in the same way as he had me. It never worked the other way round, for some reason. Maybe I didn't know him as well as he knew me.

Forced into a brave face for my parents' sake, I felt betrayed, bitter, full of anger inside even as we began our seven day break.

Yarmouth. Packed with people. The music from the amusement arcades carried on long into the night. Not the ideal place for a holiday. And it rained. The weather matched my mood.

The guest house had an electric organ, so for at least a short time I was able to lose myself in my music, while the clamour and confusion carried on around me. I felt that I was letting my parents down. This wasn't what they would have chosen. They deserved better than this. I also realised suddenly why Bill had agreed so readily to a foursome. We hardly saw him. He was up early, and off to places where he wanted to go; Stock Car Racing, Snetterton, rallies, and the like. My parents were along for the ride. Company for me.

24 July 1977

'I'm just going to get some more fags before turning in,' he said. 'Won't be five minutes.'

'I'll come with you.' I was longing to link hands and walk along the prom as I'd seen other couples do.

'No, you stay here.' He slipped out like a shadow. I didn't even see which way he went.

We went to bed at nine. It had been a tiring day. He'd been gone three hours, but I kept thinking I would hear him at any moment, creeping, like a thief, up the stairs. He'd probably gone to the pub for a quick pint I decided, as I slipped between the sheets.

By midnight, I was worried. I kept getting up to look out of the window, but could see no sign of him. I debated going out to look for him. But I was scared of being out on strange streets at night. I read for a while, but found myself reading and re-reading a page, and still not knowing what it was about.

Everyone had retired to bed. The house was silent, except for the snores from room five. I crept along the landing, and after a moment's hesitation, knocked softly on the door of room four. Muttering and scuffling within, then Dad edged open the door. When he saw my blotched face and wringing hands, he tugged me in, and we held a hurried family conference.

'But it's two in the morning, for crying out loud. Where could the lad be?'

'Oh he isn't being fair on the girl. Look how worried and upset she is!'

They showed mixed feelings as I stood, crestfallen, looking down at the carpet. If only they knew how many other evenings I'd spent out of my mind with worry. He was always disappearing, and then coming home without a word of explanation or apology.

'Has he ever done this kind of thing before?' As always, Mum was on the ball.

'Well . . . yes,' I'd been afraid to admit it.

'There you are then. He'll come back when he's good and ready.'

I couldn't stop the various possibilities flashing through my mind. Maybe he'd fallen off the jetty and been drowned? Mugged by a roving gang and lying fatally injured somewhere? Dad seemed to sense the way my mind was working.

'Look Poppet, if it will make things any easier, I'll go out and call the police if he isn't back in half an hour.'

Half an hour passed. Dad began to dress. I let loose a fresh flood of tears. Outside, feet scuffled past the door. I peeped through a crack and caught a glimpse of Bill's receding figure.

'He's back,' I announced.

'Right,' muttered Dad. 'We'll have it out here and now as to where he's been until three in the morning. What does he think he's playing at?'

I had an idea he'd enjoy hearing Bill's excuses. But Mum interjected, 'No, darling. Leave them to sort it out.' As always, she believed it wrong to intervene between husband and wife.

Back in the bedroom, Bill had retired for the night. The light was out, and he pretended to be asleep when I prodded him.

'Bill, where have you been?'

It remains an unanswered question to this day.

4 August 1977
Spent day in town after being unexpectedly awakened by Bill. Very
randy and loving. He kept tantalising me despite my pushing him
away. We came together to achieve almost heaven. It was difficult. It
took time. But it was the best for a long, long while.
I think we both felt different afterwards. We spent the morning
cuddling and kissing. Something new for us. It made me feel all warm
and loved inside, so that even the loss of my Avon collections over the
weekend faded into the background. We blew some housekeeping on
a cheesecake and eclair to celebrate. Then spent the evening watching
TV together.
It really has been a good day, and it felt so good to be alive.

Hope flared fresh within me. I felt revitalised, as if at last I had
found my lost love. I made myself believe it because I wanted so
badly to believe it. I forgot all the bad times, the angry words and
awful things that had passed between us. This was my day. I was
happy, exhilaratingly so, and I didn't mean to mar my mood with
memories. I wrote a new song.

11 August 1977
Bill took money from my purse, then turned violent after an
argument about it. My fits of dizziness and shaking have returned.

19 August 1977
Bill disappeared. After tea we were watching TV. I turned round to
speak to him and he just wasn't there. I assumed he was upstairs,
but when after half an hour or so he hadn't come back, I went to
look. His jacket had gone from the hall. He had simply slipped out
and vanished into the night.
   It reminded me of those times in the bedsit, when I had finished
washing-up after dinner and returned to his room to find him gone.
I worried myself sick until two in the morning, but decided to stay
up until he returned. My motherly instincts coming out. I had to
see him in safe and sound before I could sleep. He might have been
a wayward son, I worried over him so much.

He rolled in drunk at two-thirty. I heard him coming long before he reached the front door.

'Ssh!' I whispered, peering out into the blackness. 'Be quiet, or you'll wake the neighbours.'

'Damn the neighbours,' he yelled as loud as he could. 'They're all too bloody nosey, anyway.'

He banged the door too hard, and shattered the lower pane of glass. I automatically began sweeping up the pieces. I was terrified of what Bill would do in the mood he was in, if let loose with one of the jagged edges.

'I've been out having a drink with my Dad,' he said, by way of explanation, ' . . . and he agrees with me, I should have more money for myself, in future.'

I tried to remain calm, composed, rational. I wouldn't be drawn into an argument. But we had one anyway. He hit me across the face, shouting that I was a tight-fisted, money-pinching cunt. All I could think of were neighbours' ears listening in the night.

'Please Bill, please be quiet.'

'Sod you. I don't have to do what you say.'

'Bill . . . please.'

'Hey,' he shouted at the top of his voice. 'If you really want to know what's going on, come and take a peek at this.'

He flicked his wrist and caught me a glancing blow by my eye.

'Stop it, Bill,' I screamed.

He laughed. Punched me playfully in the stomach. Then punched me again with all the full force of his body behind it. I fell back heavily against the wall. His foot buffeted into my side. I tried to crawl away. He kicked savagely into my body again, and again, and again. Then he ran away into the night.

I sat in the kitchen contemplating a bottle of pills. What was the use of going on? Things were never going to change. I heard the door being pushed open. Was he back already? But it was Jean from next door, wakened by the noise and worried. She sat with me until four, when he returned. Sober. Not a word was said. He stomped up the stairs to bed. Jean left, taking all my tablets with her. I felt naked, helpless without them.

26 August 1977

End of a depressing week. I had fallen for an old ploy, when Bill had borrowed money on behalf of his father. Fifteen pounds we had loaned him to tide him over while he was in 'financial difficulties', as he put it. He'd collapsed at work, a heart attack they'd called it. When I'd last seen him, he'd looked old and grey.

I phoned to ask how he was, and they thanked me for the loan. 'We were glad we could pay it back with interest,' his step-mother said.

When had they paid it back? Later I asked Bill. He had already spent it. On what, he couldn't remember, or wouldn't say.

Just before our holiday, we had made friends with Kate, who lived in a ground-floor maisonette below us. Jean, next door, had her doubts about the friendship. She had heard rumours about Kate, nasty rumours, which she believed came from a reliable source. Jean warned me, 'Be careful, Jan. She's a dangerous person to know.'

Kate's answer to the accusations was, 'I make a bad enemy, but a good friend.'

Things had been going well between us. She bought items from my catalogue, and I bought from hers. We went shopping together in town, and I saw less of Jean and more of Kate. Then everything began to go wrong. Nothing I could actually specify, just suspicions. Money disappeared from my purse, which had been on the table in her kitchen while I was upstairs. But Bill had been there too—so who was to blame?

The same happened when our rent money disappeared. Bill and I had gone down to ask her to pay ours along with her own. I put the note down on the table with the rent book, and we had a coffee and a chat before leaving. Then at the door, Kate said, 'Where's the money, then?'

'I put it by the book,' I replied, and waved as we set off back home.

She rushed after us. 'There's no money there.'

We went back to see if it had slipped to the floor. But it was gone. Again, it could have been Bill or Kate.

When we went on holiday, she agreed to look after things for us.

We gave her the key. But on our return, the twenty-seven pounds I'd hidden was gone. Had Bill found it? Or had Kate taken it while we were away? There was always an element of doubt. Now she was helping us with a Council exchange with a friend of hers who wanted a maisonette. We were all set to have a house of our own at last. We couldn't wait.

28 August 1977

We moved into our new house. It was like a dream come true. For the first time, we had a front and a back garden, a place to hang the washing, and our very own dustbin. The little things seemed to matter most. Life was on the up and up. We had been as low as we could get. Now there was only one way to go.

2 September 1977

Dear Mum and Dad,

At last, I have managed to find time to write to you. It is the first chance I have had this week to even sit down and relax for half an hour or so.

We really are thrilled with our new home. Today, I spent an exciting morning hanging out our washing for the first time ever. Now we have almost all the rooms straight it looks so cosy—just like a dream come true. Then I look out of the window and see our garden, a little overgrown perhaps, surrounded by a hedge, and find it hard to believe it is all ours.

We stepped through the door on our first day here and Bill said 'Put the kettle on, love. We're home.' It sounded good. We are home. The future suddenly looks so much brighter and I even have two neighbours. Two new friends. It was only when we had anyone staying with us at the maisonette that it ever seemed to have any atmosphere. All the rows we had when we were alone convinced us that it might not only be us but the place in which we were living.

Bill takes such a new kind of pride in our new house. In fact, he has taken to shaving twice a day and wants a clean shirt and trousers every morning. I am still on my own most nights, but he does bring me home a little surprise sometimes, some present he thought I might like.

Well, I really must stop my chatter and get on with some work.

There is definitely no shortage of jobs about the house. Yesterday, I almost broke my back laying carpets. Bill had disappeared as usual. Now I have backache as well as a big plaster over the end of my thumb where I spliced nearly all the fingernail off with a Stanley knife after hitting it first with a hammer. I wish Bill had been around to help more . . .

Over the days that followed, I tried to ignore the blocked drains, the overgrown garden littered with rubbish, the grimy windows, the smell, and the little red spots that began to cover our arms and legs. Then it dawned on us that we had fleas. Perhaps this wasn't the slice of heaven we had dreamed it up to be. I scrubbed, disinfected, and cleaned the house from top to bottom. I began taking two baths a day, I felt so unclean and contaminated. Now we knew why the other couple had been so keen to move.

6 September 1977
When I hadn't heard from Kate for a while, I began to wonder about her catalogue payments. I had paid my debts with her before leaving the maisonette, but she still owed about fifty pounds on goods she had received. I decided to go and visit her the following day.

7 September 1977
Paul, Kate's husband, arrived early saying she had thrown him out. For the first time I felt really uneasy. While Bill was talking about putting Paul up for a few nights in the spare room, I ran to catch the first of two buses to see Kate.

'What are you doing here?' were the words that she greeted me with. A clear indication that something was wrong.

'Look Kate, all I'm interested in is the money you owe me for the catalogue.'

'I don't owe you a penny, but you owe me forty quid,' she countered.

I stood stunned for a moment. This was beginning to sound like a slanging match.

'But I paid you it all in full before I left.'

'Prove it.'

By now, her two daughters made a captive audience. It was true, she had omitted to sign my catalogue card. I had no proof, but I had trusted her as a friend.

'Please Kate, stop messing about. Give me the money, and I'll go.'

'Now look here, you pathetic little creature. You're a real innocent. I took you for the sucker you were, and just you try to prove I owe you money. If you dare to take it further, I shall claim I never even received the goods.'

I knew I was all the things she said I was—and more, much, much more. But was there any need for her to treat me this way?

'And furthermore,' she continued, 'I shall deny ever accepting payments from you. My catalogue will be getting in touch with you about the forty pounds.'

Suddenly, she was a witch, a woman to beware of, everything Jean and others had warned me of. I heard her ask her eldest daughter to go and get Louise, her friend. I wanted to go, to leave this house of lies. I was crying. Betrayed. I blamed myself for all that had happened. But I couldn't move. My legs refused to function.

Kate continued to talk. She told me Bill and Paul had threatened her at knife point, that they had robbed the meters and taken her money. She went on and on with her accusations, and I found my feet suddenly, and ran to the door.

'Where do you think you're going?' Louise, the woman with whom we had exchanged houses, stood on the doorstep. I tried to push past, and through a blur of tears, saw her smile—the same sadistic smile that Bill always had—as if she were enjoying my plight.

'Let me go, let me go,' I screamed.

Kate pulled me back, and slapped my face hard.

'Did you see that?' I gasped at our audience.

'She never touched you.' They answered almost in unison.

It was a conspiracy. Was this really happening to me? Kate slapped and punched, punched and slapped, until I felt blood well up in my mouth. I lashed out then, and as they stepped back from me, I ran for the door. Up the steps I ran, to Jean's. Surely she wouldn't let me down? I knocked sharply, and then keeled over against the wall. Jean opened her door, and helped me inside, fed me hot sweet tea, and called a taxi. Soon, I was home and retelling my tale of woe to Bill and Paul. Paul called the police.

'Do you wish to prefer charges?' the young constable asked, kindly.

'You bet she does,' Paul answered for me. Why hadn't it been Bill?

'Yes, yes I do,' I replied. I found talking hurt. My lower jaw was displaced. I had a cut on the inside of my mouth, and three chipped front teeth. But I thought the nightmare was over. It wasn't.

8 September 1977

The solicitor I went to see made it all sound so petty. To make matters worse, Kate's daughter still had a guitar I had loaned her, and I was told there was no hope of retrieving it, even though I could prove it was mine.

'These domestic upsets just aren't worth fighting over,' he said. 'Believe me when I say you are best leaving well alone. You could both end up being bound over to keep the peace.'

'But surely, she can't just be allowed to get away with it?' I had let too much go by default already, and I wanted to prove something to myself, as well as to her.

'Please Mrs D—. Allow me to know my job. I'm telling you, to pursue this matter would cost money, time, and effort. My advice is to leave it alone. However, she will receive a police warning, if that is any consolation.'

It wasn't. But he was the expert. He should know. I left his office, and headed for the doctor's.

I shook from head to toe in the waiting room. Every part of me was on edge. I received more tablets, together with some ominous words:

'You are about to know the differene between Depression and Acute Depression. You are suffering from shock, young lady, and I advise you to go home to bed and take a sleeping pill. Come back and see me in a few days.'

So much advice in one day! But I took the pill and was asleep within minutes.

10 September 1977
My sister Laura's wedding. The ceremony made me cry. Please
God, let her marriage be a happy one. Let her never know the
shame of being beaten, or deceived.

The buffet looked so lovely. I watched from afar, my jaw still too
painful to allow me to eat. They left in a hired car for a honeymoon
in Dorset. Suddenly, all my worries crowded in on me again, and I
began to cry.

I could have predicted what Mum's reaction would be after hearing
about Kate. 'You silly girl,' she said.

Dad was furious, and asked that I stay on with them for a while.
A break away sounded like a good idea. I agreed. I should have
stayed longer.

14 September 1977
Dearest Mum and Dad,
   *Thanks for putting up with me. Today is grey and miserable. It
matches my mood. The minute I walked through the door on
Monday evening, I felt like turning round and coming right back
again. Dirty dishes overflowed in the sink; a pan, black and burnt,
had been put on top of the fridge leaving an imprint; the bedroom
looked as if a bomb had hit it. Bill had saved no money for me, and
I had to borrow fifty pence for bus fare to get to my doctor's
appointment . . .*

I felt as if the whole world had turned against me. I wanted to shut
myself away. The smallest job demanded too much effort. In the
end, I stopped answering the doorbell or going downstairs. I lay on
the bed for most of the time, halfway between waking and sleeping.
The pills stopped me thinking, stopped me hurting inside. The only
post to come for me was from Kate's catalogue. They informed me
I had been put on their 'black list'. They demanded I pay them over
forty pounds to avoid court action. Dad replied on my behalf. They

wrote again the same as before. The thought of court hung over my
head like a great black cloud. Made me sweat.

I remained nervy, on edge. A woman answering Kate's descrip-
tion had called while I was away. I hated being alone in the house,
and dreaded what would happen if she came again.

'Please Bill, stay in with me tonight. I'm so afraid,' I'd plead.

'It's boring being in,' he'd reply, and go off to play with the band.
He was often paid fifty pounds for a performance now, but I never
saw any of it. What he spent it on I didn't know. Next night it was
always gone and he would come begging to me for more.

I lay in bed for most of every day, listening to the traffic, children
going to school, the milkman, the children coming home from
school, and the evening rush hour. The house was a tip, and I
didn't care. No-one else cared, so why should I? Bill had only to
speak to me, and I would burst into tears. He took what he wanted
from my purse. When it was empty, he knew there was no more.

21 September 1977

Found out through a letter in the post that Bill was in arrears with
payments on a loan I didn't even know he had.

22 September 1977

Bill spent all the bills' money due to be paid next week.

26 September 1977

On another course of tranquillisers from the doctor. Being literally
sick with worry. Start of weekly appointments again.

28 September 1977

Bill stayed off work because he had no money for bus fares.

3 October 1977

Today marked the beginning of my road to recovery. It began when

I heard a child crying bitterly outside the window. 'Mummy, Mummy, where are you?'

It came to me through a fog of despair. A cry I would like to have made myself, only it would have meant defeat. They thought they had won. I wasn't beaten yet.

I dragged myself out of bed, and sat by the window looking out at the world—grey, cold, miserable and uninviting. I wanted desperately to crawl back beneath the safety of the sheets. Only I had to face the world again. I made myself believe it was a challenge. If I didn't help myself, no-one else would.

4 October 1977

The next day, I washed and brushed my teeth for the first time in weeks. It took time to pick the pieces of me off the floor and put myself back together again.

From then on I did each day what I had done the day before, and added something new, until I had myself downstairs eating breakfast. Then I started on the house.

'You're up, then.' Bill said, incredulously when he arrived home one night. He looked as though a small miracle had taken place, and was fast to take advantage. 'Have you a pound or two you can lend me?'

Things were back to normal or very nearly.

Weeks later my health still wasn't good. I suffered from dizzy spells. My legs would give way, making me sit down suddenly. Migraines fogged my mind. Mum and Dad were worried sick. They made the trip down from Birmingham almost every week to see how I was. To take me out of myself for a while. But I kept slipping back.

They had no conception of what my life was really like, and I was ashamed. I blamed myself for things going wrong. Laura, my sister, was practical, sensible, all the things I was not—a daughter to be proud of. She and Ralph were buying their own house. They had all their plans neatly packaged, and tied up with string. I tried to imagine her in my situation—she would have left long ago, not stuck it out for four long years. So why did I? What kind of a fool was I to come back for more, and more, and more?

6 October 1977
Bill brought home £9 for a week's wages. I wished I knew where all his money was going.

10 October 1977
Put on new course of stronger nerve tablets.

13 October 1977
Week's wages of £10.

5 November 1977
Bill took money from my purse for a night out.

14 November 1977
A car pulled up outside the house. I didn't recognise the man who walked up the path. Another debt collector?

'Mrs D—? I'm afraid I have some bad news. Shall we go inside?'

My legs were already collapsing under me. It had to be a summons for bills in arrears, a bailiff—or worse?

'Your husband has had an accident at work. He's at the hospital now, and in shock. They want to do an emergency operation. I can take you there now, if you like.'

He had to steady me as we walked towards the car. My head was reeling. What new crisis had fate in store for me?

Bill looked pale and shaky. He took my hand in his, and held it for a long while. He smiled lopsidedly, and I knew he needed me more now than ever before. Still with no idea of what was really wrong, I waited at his bedside as he was taken into surgery. A sister had tried to explain earlier, but her words had fused together and I hadn't taken them in.

When I next saw him, his hand was heavily bandaged and held

upright by a splint. He had ground his finger instead of the piece of metal he was working on, and would be off work for a month. I didn't dare think of the consequences, or dwell on the worries crowding my mind. I went home, took two sleeping pills, and slept.

15 November 1977
Two policemen arrived on the doorstep. Both looked very formal, and very official. It took some moments for me to open the door.

'Good morning. Is this the residence of William James D—?'

'Yes . . . yes, that's right.' Net curtains moved in the houses over the road. The neighbours were having a field day.

'May we speak to him?'

'I'm sorry, he isn't in. I mean, he's in hospital.' The two exchanged glances, and I explained the situation.

'Well, thank you, Mrs. D—' They began to walk away.

'Look, can I help?' I asked. I was only the wife, but I felt I should know what was wrong.

'We wanted to see his driving papers. As you are probably aware, he was pulled up last week for having no tax and insurance. We'll call again.'

On that ominous note, I shut the door, and wobbled to a chair. When I'd stopped shaking enough to write, I made a list of all we owed. It came to the staggering total of £908.21, and that was without this latest incident, or any other HPs, and fines I didn't know about. Almost one thousand pounds in debt. I made some hot sweet tea, and sat down to contemplate our gloomy future.

16 November 1977
Bill came home from hospital.

23 November 1977
The police came back. Fine of forty pounds.

26 November 1977
I found a crumpled letter, dated some weeks previously, at the back of a drawer. It demanded that the balance on an outstanding loan taken out for a Ford Zephyr car, registration number — be paid in full within twenty-eight days, or action would be taken. My mind went back to the day I had commented on the car outside, and found it to be his. I had always assumed that the two hundred pounds that went missing from our savings at the same time, had gone on it. I could only boggle at what he might have bought with such a large sum of money.

1 December 1977
I felt so unhappy, so insecure and neglected.

It seemed as if I had a boy for a husband, not a man, and an unreliable, unfeeling, selfish boy at that. After doing all the worrying and running about for both of us for money to survive while he was off—phoning Social Security to enquire about Industrial Injuries Benefit and the like, then taking my place at the back of a long, long queue—all I received in return was a nod and a shrug. He didn't care. He thought things would right themselves on their own.

I got upset, and started to cry. All he could do was laugh. How could he be so callous and cruel? Then he grabbed the rest of the money from my purse, saying he was going to collect his one day's wages from work.

I was due to sing at a concert, but had no way of getting there without bus fare. I said as much, and had the money thrown at me along with a metal ashtray. It caught me on the cheek, leaving a vivid welt.

5 December 1977
First try at sex for months.

9 December 1977
Bill disappeared for the day. Left house at 8.00 am saying he

wouldn't be long. Arrived home at 10.30 p.m. Row!

20 December 1977
As a child this was my favourite time of year. I bucked myself up
by decorating the house, and cooking pies and cakes. But marzipan,
mincemeat, and marshmallows kept disappearing from the cupboard. Then chocolates from the tree—the best ones shaped like
Santa, with cream inside. My favourites—and it seemed like Bill's
too, only he couldn't wait.

I had bought a hamper from the catalogue, and now I lovingly
undid the string to drool over the goodies, and put the things away
in the larder. My hand delved into the box, but came away with
nothing but straw packing. Empty. Where was all the food? I
turned the carton over. It had been opened from the bottom.

'What about the hamper then, Bill?' I asked later.

'Oh that, you found it then,' he replied off-handedly. His don't
care attitude infuriated me.

'I found it all right—empty. What the hell did you do with it all?
Flog it?'

'No. As a matter of fact, I ate it. I took a tin or two to share with
my mates at work. I owed them. They'd lent me money, and I
needed something to fob them off with, while I got cash together to
pay them.'

What could I say? I couldn't bring it back. My nails dug painfully
into the palm of my hand. I wanted so badly to let rip, to wipe that
sardonic smile from his face. I wanted to lash out. To hit him
where it would hurt. I think I hated him most of all then. It had
taken so much effort and will-power to get the hamper. Now it had
been all for nothing.

'What's the big deal, anyway? It was only food.'

I slammed out of the room, pounded up the stairs, and packed
my case. 'You're leaving then, are you?' He stood at the door,
smoking. 'Where will you be going?' He had the upper hand, and
he knew it. I thought of my sisters, my parents preparing for
Christmas. They would have plans of their own. I couldn't spoil it
for them. I couldn't leave now.

My case remained packed. I pretended it was my warning, my

deterrent against further abuse. But I didn't fool him. I didn't even deceive myself.

21 December 1977
We went to a party. The other three members of the band were there with their girlfriends. It was one of those boozy affairs where the drink flowed freely. I set out to enjoy myself, but soon found I was sitting alone. I listened to the girls talking about fashion, make-up, work. My interests were books, writing, photography, folk music. What had we in common? I felt much older than twenty-four.

'And what have you been doing with yourself, Jan?' The question came in one of those awful silences, so that all eyes were on me. I blushed, and Bill laughed drunkenly. I felt like the joke everyone was laughing at.

'Oh, nothing special,' I said, as airily as I could; as though it didn't matter, but my voice gave me away. It mattered a whole lot. It hurt like hell that I wasn't making more of myself.

'Have another drink.' Johnny leaned over to refill my glass. His other arm was latched around Dee. They all looked so happy, merry, looking forward to Christmas. I glanced over at Bill, pouring liquor down his throat as if it were water. Then I rushed from the room. I didn't belong here. I wasn't one of them. I was Me. I just hadn't found myself properly yet. All I had were dreams.

'We'll have to be going,' I announced to the assembly on my return.

'Mummy says, does she?' Bill chanted from the far corner. He refused to budge. I sat out another half hour. Others began to move. Then I saw how drunk Bill really was, as he lurched forward, dropping his glass.

'Please, can someone give me a lift?' I asked. 'I don't want to go home with Bill.'

There was a stunned silence. Someone said, 'Oh come on, don't be silly. He's your husband.'

'I know,' I countered, 'and I don't want to go home with him.'

It sounded ludicrous. He wasn't the only one the worse for drink, but I knew he alone would be violent with it.

'You can both come with me,' Johnny offered. 'I'll drop you off at the chippy at the top of your road.' I still wasn't happy, but with the last bus having gone a couple of hours ago, I couldn't afford to say no.

I became more and more upset the nearer home we got. I told Bill he could go to the chip shop and I'd see him back at the house. But he dragged me along, and for good measure, pushed me in front of him. It was raining, the pavements were wet, and I slipped and sat down hard in a puddle.

'Oh come on, Jan, gerrup. I'm gerring wet.' He was acting as if it were all my fault, and to my annoyance, I found myself crying. The more I cried, the madder he became. In the chip shop, he started shouting and swearing.

'Bill, stop it. You're making a complete fool of yourself.'

He shouted all the louder, and they served us quickly so that we would go. I followed ashamed and embarrassed as he wobbled down the centre of the road, trying to follow the white lines. Cars hooted as they passed, and headlamps spotlit us out of the shadows.

At home, he upset his chip supper over the settee, then set fire to a chair with his cigarette. When drunk he needed watching constantly if an accident was to be prevented, yet he hated having me around.

'Get outta the way,' he yelled.

I receded to the far corner, but rushed forward as a second cigarette set a piece of the carpet alight.

'Let's go to bed,' I pleaded.

He lashed out and the usual session of violence started. As I tried to evade his grasp, it was as if he had a hundred tentacles. He reached out and twisted my arm painfully behind my back, all the time thudding his knee into the small of my back. It made me scream with the sheer agony of it. I thought he would break my arm.

'Bill . . . for pity's sake.'

He maintained a monotonous thud, thud, thud. I tried to twist round, but his grip was too tight. He laughed. I cried.

I felt my head suddenly being yanked back. He had hold of my hair. Then he let go without warning so that I fell to the floor. In the interval that followed he lit a cigarette. I watched his eyes try to focus on the end of it. It took several attempts before it was lit. Silence. He stared mutely at me. Smoking. Waiting. Watching for my next move. I dared not aggravate the situation.

I didn't speak. I didn't dare even look in his direction. I tried to get up slowly. It was like dealing with a dangerous animal. My knees knocked together. My right arm, the one he had twisted, was numb. Then pins and needles began to shoot up and down it as the circulation returned. I gasped, falling backwards, and knocked painfully against the fireplace surround. It caught my knee and shoulder. For a few minutes I was blinded by tears. Still we maintained a stony silence.

When I dared to look at Bill he was laughing. I was shaking from head to toe. My teeth chattered. My arms flopped. I felt sapped of strength. Bill dropped the cigarette he was holding. In his drunken state he had to bend right down to focus properly on the floor. I heaved myself up and made a rush for the door and the stairs. I barricaded myself in the spare room for the night.

'Happy Christmas,' I whispered, as I cuddled a teddy bear to keep warm.

'Happy Christmas.'

1978

I had wanted to leave my marriage for years . . . It was never any good—not from the beginning. But I deformed my mind to believing it was. I told myself nothing better was possible. I convinced myself that sadness and compromise were the ways of the world.

ERICA JONG

2 January 1978
Bill didn't go to work because he would have had to walk. No buses on Bank Holiday.

8 January 1978
I was living in a kind of limbo. I was no longer a part of the world going on around me. I sat in the back seat of the car, listening to the two in front, talking trivialities, trying to keep my homecoming a happy occasion. The car sped through the busy streets back to my home and Bill. I tried to keep my mind on what Laura and Ralph were saying, and not think of the awful mess I might find awaiting me. It had been good to be away from it for a while. Birmingham had offered the santuary I needed.

I felt old, too old. I could not shake off this dreamlike state. It was the pills, I supposed. But the doctor had said on my last visit, 'They're what's holding you together, my dear. Without them you would be a mess. You'd simply fall apart and become a nervous wreck.'

We were approaching the outskirts of the town. Laura and Ralph fell silent. My knees began to shake. My stomach churned. We drew up outside the house. The white Zephyr had been driven off the road on to the overgrown garden, away from the prying eyes of the police. Bill still had no tax, no insurance, no licence to drive, and had incurred another forty-pound fine only the week before. But the car remained his prize possession. He meant to keep it.

I could put off the moment no longer. Ralph was already unloading my luggage, and I could see Bill's face peering out of an upstairs window. He opened the front door as I came up the path, and I slowly re-entered my prison.

I made myself ignore the mess. Dirty dishes hid the sink. The living room carpet was spotted with ash. I stopped myself from bending to clean it. The bin was full of chip papers, the bed upstairs grimy and unmade. He stank. He no longer bothered to bath when he came home full of factory smells and sweat. I sat down on the edge of the bed and cried.

10 January 1978

I felt a hollow emptiness inside. I had no tears left to cry. I forced myself to get up and face another day. The weeks stretched darkly, interminably ahead. I had lost all hope.

The lady next door knocked. I didn't answer. The milkman called for payment. I didn't answer, but watched him through a crack in the closed curtains. The minutes ticked by while I sat reading last year's diary. Hope began to creep back. This would be my year. The year I rose up against oppression. Found myself. I didn't know how or when. But I decided my time would come.

18 January 1978

The day before our fourth wedding anniversary. Bill didn't go to work. It was his fifth day off in three weeks, and he had been warned that if his absences continued, he would be sacked. He shrugged his shoulders in the face of authority.

'How can they expect me to go without money for fags or bus fare?' As usual, his argument was totally irrational.

'What about the money from your last gig?' I don't know why I bothered to ask.

'Oh, that went ages ago.' He no longer felt he had to justify himself. What he did with his money was his affair alone.

'But you only got it on Saturday. Still, if you insist on staying at home, you needn't expect me to be here to cook for you.' I, too, had changed. I was sticking to the resolution I had made. This year things would be different.

'Where are you going?'

'Around.' I tried to adopt his don't care attitude. He hated that. He loved to see me caring, crying, worried. Inside, I was all of those things, and more. But he couldn't see inside my head. I put on my coat.

'What time will you be back?'

'Depends.' I remained non-commital, uncooperative, and decided to dress up as if I really were going somewhere special. This made Bill nervy, on edge, worried. It was like playing out a game of chess, with him on the defensive.

'Checkmate,' I muttered, as I slammed the door behind me, and ran for the bus.

I sat, huddled over a cup of cold coffee, re-assessing the Situations Vacant. Outside looked bleak and uninviting. Snowflakes fell on people rushing by. I was putting off the moment when I would have to join them in the cold. Then my eyes fixed on an advert I had missed:

Receptionist wanted for busy
Hairdressing Salon in centre of town.

I read the small print. Excitement welled up inside me. This had to be it! Please God, let it be it.

I began walking towards the bus, but on impulse, diverted from my route, and went instead into a small boutique boasting a closing-down sale. I spent a long time trying on and choosing what to buy. Finally I settled on a new coat and skirt with matching blouse, different from my usual style. I paid for them with the gas bill money and, pleased with my purchases, I headed home.

Bill was out, and for once I was glad. I didn't want him to see my new clothes. I noticed as I sat down with pen and paper in hand, that he had tidied up before he'd left. But I resisted the urge to dwell on the rare occurrence. I had no misconceptions about what it could mean—Bill needed money.

I posted my letter, and arrived back at the same time as Bill. He carried a battered guitar case. I held myself back from asking where he had been. His face showed he was in an evil mood. I escaped upstairs to change. He came after me. He was obsessed with the need for money.

'They wouldn't buy my old guitar, not even in a second-hand shop. I'm desperate, Jan. Just give me a pound or two.'

'I'd like to Bill, but I haven't more than fifty pence myself.' I averted my eyes from the drawer containing the remainder of the gas bill money.

'Where did you go, anyway?' He hated not knowing, and I wasn't about to tell him, not until I had the job, anyway.

'I had business in town to attend to,' I said importantly.

He started shaking me by the shoulders. His nails dug into my flesh. My head was rocked back and forth, to and fro. My teeth chattered. My jaw ached. I felt like I was being snapped in two. He pushed me down. Dragged me across the floor. The disobedient servant would bow before the master.

'You animal. Keep off me. You won't get a penny.'

'Bitch!' His hand hit my cheek. My head jolted back. I wriggled out from under him. Slapped him as hard as I could across the face with the flat of my hand. I was angry. For perhaps the first time, I was mad.

'Keep away, you brute. You're not getting anything from me.' It was as if my secret gave me an inner power to rise up and resist.

I made for the door, but he was too quick for me. The side of his face was red, his pride, his masculinity badly dented. He grabbed hold of my legs in a rugby tackle.

'Go away. Go away. Go away.'

It sounded feeble. Weak. A child's chant. Why was it I could never think of suitably hurtful phrases to use? I was sobbing, gasping for air. I couldn't get any into my lungs quickly enough.

'Get away from me. You pig. You animal. You fucking bloody bastard. Fuck off!' I kicked him in the chest. There was just time for a moment's satisfaction. He gasped. I had hurt him. He pulled my feet from under me. I crashed to the floor.

'I'll fucking beat your hide off for that, you little bitch.' Arms wound around me like rope, crushing me. I found it difficult to get my breath. To breathe. My chest heaved. My head swam. Blackness threatened to engulf me. I felt myself sinking into oblivion. I tried to get an arm free, but he held it in a vice. My teeth sank into his wrist.

'You little wildcat, you bitch. You'll pay for that.' Fists hammered against my head. The room was swimming in circles around me. He batted my head against the wall like a ball. All the time he stayed just out of reach of my hands. Then he let me go, abruptly, and ran out of the house.

Slowly, the merry-go-round in my head stopped revolving. The head pains, headaches, and dizziness stayed with me for days. When I tried to comb my hair, I found painful bumps on my scalp. I hurt all over. Yet I could not tell my doctor. I was still too ashamed to admit to being beaten. In the past well-meaning friends had advised me to hit back. 'Don't just sit there and take it. Hit him harder where it hurts.' Now I had done so and I wore the scars to prove it. He had never beaten me so brutally, cruelly, as now. The scars would be with me for a long time to come.

2 February 1978

Bill began bouncing cheques in desperation. Another fine for driving without tax, insurance, and licence; this time for eighty pounds. Another hundred-pound loan from a naïve finance company for a newer, bigger, better amplifier. Daily reminders for previous court fines, HP arrears, loan payments. A bounced cheque to *Reader's Digest* for a record.

At the same time good news for me. I'd got the job.

I had almost ducked out at the last moment. Fifty candidates had applied for the post, and the six who sat buffing their painted nails when I arrived for my first interview had looked cool, composed, confident. I took my place in the queue, and listened to a blue-eyed blonde boasting of her past experience.

'Of course, I know only too well the kind of person they'll be after. It isn't everyone who can do this work. It takes drive, initiative.'

Her name was called next, and she clip-clopped into the office, only to emerge again after a few minutes, her bright red lips firmly drawn together. Without a word, she passed us and was gone. A heavy silence fell over the remaining few. One by one, we were ushered into the inner sanctum, and one by one we left.

'You have to become part of a team. Would you mind if we re-modelled, re-shaped the outer you?' they asked, when it was my turn.

'No,' I replied. 'I wanted a change anyway.' The only thing I stipulated was they didn't dye my hair.

The salary was good. They wanted someone with no pre-conceived ideas about the job. I would be looking after the books, and it might mean staying on after the others had left to balance them correctly.

'Are you prepared to do overtime?' they asked.

'Yes, of course,' I replied simply. It would give me an excuse not to return home until Bill had left for the evening.

I was bubbling over with enthusiasm and I wanted to tell Bill all about it, meant him to be pleased too. But a film was on TV, and in the end, I gave up trying to compete. It pricked my bubble a little, and I felt deflated. He did buy me a small tin of spaghetti for a celebration supper, but I would have liked it a lot better if he'd given me a little more attention.

14 February 1978
First morning of my new job. Valentine's Day. No cards, not even from Bill. It would have been a real boost when my nerves were jangling. There was so much to do, to learn at work. I floundered along in a fog.

22 February 1978
Bill still hadn't paid court fines, despite him telling me he had.

27 February 1978
Dear Mum and Dad,
   This is the first chance I have really had of writing you a newsy letter. Things have been very hectic this last couple of weeks.
   Our day begins at six. It is awful to hear the alarm; and to know that Time is the master. Breakfast is a mug of tea, and a slice of toast, then Bill leaves for work at seven. I now have to spend a full half hour solely on make-up and nails, after a rather embarrassing demonstration at Boots. Everyone leered at me while I was being painted. It is so much more trouble than my usual splash of cream and coat of powder.
   I am usually the first to arrive at the Salon. There are customer bills to be made in readiness, telephone calls to answer, and pages and pages of bookwork. The bosses seem to have a mania for wanting to know how many trims, cut and blow drys, perms and colours each assistant has done in a day. A system for doing this was devised by the boss's son who is slowly taking over the business, but it needs constant checks and re-checks. My head is reeling by the end of the day, and my feet feel like two blocks of lead.

28 February 1978
Bill kept hitting me when we tried unsuccessfully to have sex.

March 1978
It was fine at first me working. Then arguments flared at home.
   'Where's my shirt for tonight? I need a clean one to wear on stage.'
   'I'm sorry, love. I haven't had time to do it.' I couldn't rid myself of the overpowering tiredness I felt at night.
   But Bill had no sympathy. 'Oh come on, get off your butt and do some work. You don't know the meaning of the word. My job's twice as gruelling as yours, mentally and physically.'
   I was too tired to argue.
   He laid into me eventually, for leaving the dishes in the sink. Feeling guilty about the housework going to pot, I spent two nights washing, hoovering, cleaning and cooking. Then, next day, I flaked

out at work.

Bill decided to help out.

'Don't bother about the shopping this week,' he said. 'I'll do it.' His shopping consisted of buying a couple of tins of meat and veg before stopping off for a pint at the pub. The housekeeping was drunk along with the bills money. I began to feel as if I were slowly killing myself doing everything, yet I couldn't trust him long enough to share the jobs needing to be done.

We took part in a survey on relationships. We completed the questionnaires separately, and Bill sealed his in a large brown envelope ready to post, before leaving for work. Unable to resist, I took a peek at his answers, wondering why he had been so shy about sharing them with me. Reading them was a revelation!

He freely admitted he could find nothing good in our marriage, and that we were constantly bickering and I was not surprised to read that he resented any control, on my part, over his money and the way that he spent it. Our sexual incompatability I had also thought he would be honest about. But I was surprised to see that he fancied group orgies, and would like to see me doing it with someone else. This upset me, although I realised that this was one time he had been completely open, and free with his thoughts. He'd rated our happiness as almost zero, and had even stated that, given his chances over again, he would not marry.

The truth hurt.

Nothing was going right for me at work or home. I was in a mess both physically and emotionally. My concentration wavered. Often I was still at the Salon three hours after everyone else had left, trying desperately to balance the books.

'Pull yourself together, for heaven's sake,' the boss began to tell me almost daily.

1 April 1978

I couldn't do a thing right. Everyone seemed to have complaints. Then around midday, life suddenly got very hectic and I found myself in one hell of a mess. Customers clamoured for attention.

Clients hovered, waiting to pay their bills. The phone refused to stop ringing, and my head still hurt where Bill had struck me the previous night. By dinner, my mind seemed to have blown into a million pieces.

I was tired when I reached home, but Bill did nothing to help. He went out to play with Hot Ayr, leaving me crying upstairs in a pigsty of a house. I felt so low, so unloved and uncared for.

12 April 1978
I found a letter Bill had written in reply to an advertisement. He was looking for a flat. I confronted him with it when he came home from work.

'But Jan, you can see our marriage is a farce. We're just pretending, playing at being in love.'

For the first time in four years, we sat down and talked rationally about our crumbling relationship. We were communicating. We decided to split. Bill freely confessed he had known I was near to breaking point, and had been preparing to make a run for it. Now, he decided it would be better for us to make it a mutual agreement of separation, so that I couldn't divorce him anyway. He was scared of the legal hassle. I agreed to go along with his wishes.

13-28 April 1978
I plodded around, telling everyone we were separating, that I was going to Birmingham to be with my parents. I visited the bank, the doctor, the Council, a solicitor, Social Security, and numerous other official sources to clarify my position. They all said the same:

'But Mrs D—, you are the one who is leaving. You are technically deserting your husband, your marriage. As such, you will be entitled to nothing—no help from the State.'

At least, I knew where I stood. It was going to be a long, uphill climb from here on in.

In the evenings we calmly made out lists, dividing up the furniture and household goods between us. At work, I was being sick, having dizzy spells, and shaking uncontrollably. The pills didn't seem to help. Ironically, Bill was the best he had ever been.

He made dinner for me, and made sure I was comfortable before he left to play at a gig at night. He became kindness itself now that I was leaving.

On our last night together, he took me out.

'To celebrate,' he said. 'To celebrate our freedom, our liberation.'

The war was over.

28 April 1978

Laura and Ralph arrived. They were to drive me to Mum and Dad's, where I hoped to stay until I had straightened myself out.

'A separation will do you both a power of good,' Mum had said, when she first heard.

'It will give you both time to think things over, and see things in a new light,' mused Dad.

They both had the idea that this was only a temporary measure. Some kind of holiday, after which we would come together again.

29 April 1978

The day began in a golden haze of sunshine. It was hot and humid, and I decided on impulse to wear my new summer outfit, bought with last week's wages. Bill had accused me of being frivolous with my money.

'Why don't you put your mind to paying off some of these fines and loans? You've complained enough about them in the past.'

'But they're not mine to pay,' I'd countered.

'We're still man and wife,' he'd been quick to point out. 'What's yours is mine, and what's mine is yours.'

The words were right, but somehow the meaning was all wrong.

Everyday thoughts began to flash through my mind. I put the kettle on, made tea, and tiptoed upstairs to the stirring sleepers. I almost tripped over my suitcase and guitar on the landing. Suddenly, they brought it all back, and my hands shook uncontrollably as I handed the cups to Laura and Ralph. Today was the day I was leaving my marriage.

The date had been ringed in red on the calendar for a couple of weeks. Now it had actually arrived. I could hardly believe it. I felt strangely empty as, for the umpteenth time, I checked my list of things I was taking with me. I had expected to feel at least something, maybe even cry a little regretfully over what had been, and why it should have come to this. I looked around the house, the place I had once thought of as home, and felt like a stranger. I just wanted to get on with what I had to do.

I couldn't help feeling a failure as we packed ourselves into the car. Bill didn't even bother to say goodbye. But it didn't matter. Nothing mattered now, except to get away to a new town, and strangers who wouldn't know.

May 1978
Mum and Dad were bitter, angry. They couldn't understand or accept. They just wanted to welcome me back into the sheltering folds of the family, to protect me from being hurt again.

Unknown to them I cried for the past. Alone in my bed at night, I mourned the loss of my husband and home. I pined for a place of my own, and someone to share the rest of my life with. I found it hard to let go, to cut free from what had been, and I counted the days since my leaving. I even wondered at one point if I should go back.

Everything seemed such an almighty hassle. I had to fight for every smallest thing. The meanest of battles became a major victory. I had no money. I queued for what seemed like hours at the Unemployment Office, only to be given a sheaf of forms. Shakily my hand hovered over the blank boxes, and my foggy mind tried to find answers. Then I took my place again at the back of another queue.

'But you haven't filled in sections D, E F, H, or J,' stated the lady behind the counter.

'I can't,' I replied simply.

'Oh come, they're simple enough.'

I felt like a fool, with everyone else listening.

'Now then, which category do you come under . . . single, married, divorced, or widowed?' She wanted to file me, slot me into a place in her card index, a number instead of a name.

'Actually, I'm still officially married, but separated from my husband at this time,' I tried to make it as simple for her as possible.

'I see,' she said, icily. I watched her scribble in the margin. 'He left you, I take it?'

'No. The other way round. I left him.'

Why did I suddenly feel so guilty, so ashamed of leaving my loveless marriage?

'Now,' she said, leaving that section and moving swiftly on to the next, 'How many children have you?'

'None,' I replied, and looked down at the floor.

'Well, have you a doctor's certificate then, with a reason as to why you shouldn't work?' She was getting desperate. She obviously disliked being unable to categorise me, to file me away, and shut the drawer on my life.

'No,' I whispered. 'I haven't been to the doctor's yet.'

She told me to report back in a couple of days time, and marked me down as a large, ominous question mark. I crept away quietly to cry.

I sat in the doctor's waiting room that evening, while waves of self-pity washed over me. My mind kept working over the same ground. I was still gnawing at the problem of how to breathe life into a dead marriage. If I took over all the money, and paid the bills . . . If I could instill into myself a cool, level head, and blanket out the emotion underneath . . . But I knew deep down it wasn't up to me to change.

I moved to a chair at the side of the doctor's desk. I was shaking like a leaf, and absentmindedly kept lifting the gold band on and off my finger, as if my mind was still asking 'will I go, or won't I?'

'Now, what can I do for you, young lady?'

He was my father's doctor, and I didn't know what to say. 'I've just left my husband. I was on anti-depressants . . . could you give me something to stop me hurting inside?' The words spilled out, muddled and confused. It wasn't what I had been going to say at all. I had had it all planned, and now I had even made a mess of this.

'Come, come. Everyone has their ups and downs. Go home like a good wife, and kiss and make up.' He didn't understand.

I tried again, 'But he hits me. It took a great deal for me to leave, and now I've taken this step, I don't want to go back—not really. Please, all I need are some pills, and a form for the Unemployment.'

I was crying. He motioned me to the changing room, and examined me on the couch. I breathed in and out. He tapped my chest several times over, took my pulse.

'You seem fit enough to me,' he pronounced. 'I can't find anything physically wrong with you.'

I ran out then, to Dad waiting patiently in the car. His comforting arm around my shoulders brought forth a fresh flood of tears.

'He told me to go back, to go home . . .'

Dad didn't wait to hear more. He stormed into the surgery to tear a strip off an astonished receptionist and doctor.

We returned home in silence. I ran up to my room. Downstairs, I could hear Mum and Dad having a heated discussion. Tempers were flaring, and I wished I hadn't come. I should have tried to settle things without involving my parents. They just didn't know what had hit them. Dad looked as if he had aged ten years. A separation was halfway to a divorce, and obviously to be frowned upon; something nasty to be swept under the carpet, conveniently out of sight. I felt ashamed of having disgraced the family name.

The doctor did give me a certificate eventually, and renewed it every seven days for a month. The same word was on it each time—anxiety. Such a trite word for such a major event in my life. I took it to the lady at the Unemployment, who accepted it coolly. She filed it away with the question mark—but still I had no money.

The Social Security interviewed me in a private office. '. . . by law, whether a couple be separated mutually or otherwise, a man must maintain his wife by weekly payments of £13.05,' a Liable Relatives Officer quoted at me, and smiled. It sounded simple, but like any other payment Bill had made, it would be in arrears. Then where would I be? They called it 'maintenance', but added as an afterthought:

'It's a pity in a way, that there are no children involved. A child or two would have helped.'

'Helped whom?' I asked no-one in particular.

One week after leaving home, I travelled back with Ralph and my younger sister's boyfriend Tony. We pulled up outside the house in a van, and prepared to put my half of the furniture on board. I had mixed feelings about seeing Bill again and I felt physically sick as I knocked timidly at the door.

'Come in, everything's ready,' he greeted me like a stranger. His face was hard, and his eyes seemed to stare right through me. The moment I saw him, I knew whatever we had had between us was over. It was the parting of the ways.

Bill sat on the bottom stair, while Ralph and Tony traipsed backwards and forwards with furniture. He raised no objections, and made only one comment the entire time we were there, 'You know, I'm actually enjoying this!'

I eased past him to stand for the last time in the room that had been our bedroom. It seemed fitting that it should begin and end here. I averted my eyes from the bed, to gaze bleakly out of the window. A crowd of onlookers had gathered outside, hovering like vultures around the van. I turned away. On a chair, sat a pile of photograph albums. The top one was open at our wedding, but every picture with Bill in it had been removed. The other pages had been dealt with likewise. It was as if he were trying to blank himself out of the past. I was empty of emotion as I headed for the front door. I turned for the last time, and caught Bill's eye. There were no regrets, no tears, no embrace. We smiled, we waved, and I whispered goodbye.

Now I had my own things around me, and could sleep in my own bed. But still it was difficult, so different from my normal routine. Instead of enjoying the freedom, such as it was, I hated it. I missed my cheery milkman, missed being in my own home with a back door and garden. I kept catching myself thinking of what I would usually have been doing.

Too many memories crowded my mind, so at times I felt like screaming to make the world understand how I felt. Mum and Dad did their best, but they tended to think that while they were around to help put me together again, to look after me, things could only get better. They might have in time, but I knew I had to make the effort to try for myself.

It was strange how I began to blank out the bad times, and think only of the good. I felt so alone, isolated, rejected, betrayed. It was like being the black sheep of the family, constantly having to hear apologies and excuses made on my behalf. I had brought shame on my family, and the guilt lay heavy on my shoulders.

Mum and Dad began to draw a veil over what had been. They introduced me into their social circles as their single daughter, and glossed over the past. I hid my gold band in company, but wore it in private. I was loath to give up my status as a married woman. I learned to make do with threesomes, always being one of a crowd, and never being left alone for long. Everyone was falling over themselves to make me feel wanted, but it had the opposite effect. I started to feel stifled, hemmed in. I took to walking, cycling, playing tennis, taking my frustrations out on the ball. It became part of my campaign to tire myself out, so that at night, I was too tired to think.

My doctor had congratulated me before I left home. 'This is the break you needed,' he'd said. 'All it needs is time, and you will be like a new woman.'

Time was now something I had in abundance. I had expected everything to come right as soon as I left; for my health to return, my shaking to stop, and the man of my dreams to come into my life to give me that happy-ever-after ending. But it was all taking so long.

I walked along a busy Birmingham street on a sunny Saturday afternoon, and saw only things I didn't want to see. It hurt when a couple passed holding hands, with obvious love and happiness shining on their faces. I wondered if I'd ever feel the same way. An ache started deep down inside me as a smiling baby bumped past me in a pram. Yet I still remembered Bill's words as we'd decided to split, 'You know, I wouldn't let you go if we had a child. You'd be mine for all time then.'

I had that to be thankful for, at least. I was glad I hadn't got pregnant.

Relatives wrote, sending their condolences, wished me well for the future, and then went on to say how they'd wondered why it hadn't happened sooner. They covered their emotions behind a mask of words. I felt as if I was on trial; that they were judge and jury over our marriage. I found I was considered a threat by other married couples. The few friends I'd had in Birmingham dropped me the moment I returned. I was an outcast, betrayed by my own kind. Even those who'd promised to keep in touch, didn't.

Over the weeks that followed, I began to fall into a decline. I lived in a state of suspended animation. I walked around in a dream. Figures floated past me in a mist. I refused to see beyond myself and my depression. I withdrew totally from the world. My tablets were my lifeline. They stopped me hurting, and switched off my mind from memories. I got up most days at midday and walked aimlessly around. I played the piano, sang songs of women lamenting their loved ones. Drifted from day to day.

June 1978
Mum and Dad took me away on holiday with them to Portsmouth. Ralph and Laura came too. It was good to get away and slowly I felt myself come alive again. I found new interests to occupy my time, and when I returned to Birmingham I started looking for a job. My term of mourning for the death of my marriage was at an end.

I visited a solicitor to start divorce proceedings, and on his advice, I made a list from my diaries of past events. It was the first time I had allowed myself to dwell on them since I'd left, and they made heavy reading. Friends had told me to just up and go. I had no children to keep me there—so why had I stayed? Perhaps I had lived on hope for so long, that it was difficult to give up, to admit defeat and myself and my marriage a failure.

I had a new kind of gleam in my eyes these days. Mum noticed it, and watched me looking at all the eligible bachelors who passed my way. There was the young man in the park, whom I just happened to sit by after a particularly gruelling game of tennis.

'Lovely day,' I began, casually.

'Yes, and you looked as if you were having a great game on the courts,' he replied.

He'd noticed me. I blushed, and tried to cover my confusion with a question, 'Do you play?'

'Oh, I used to. But now I always seem so busy.'

He began to tell me about his love for photography, and I enthused with him. Then after about half an hour, he looked at his watch. I wondered for a fleeting moment if he was about to ask to see me again, arrange a date—another time, another place.

'Heavens, my wife will be getting worried.' He brought me down to earth with a bump. 'It's been nice talking to you, but I really must go. She's expecting our third child, you know.'

My dream was shattered.

'You don't want to fall for the first man who shows you some attention,' Mum said, afterwards. 'You'll only come to grief, and end up making a complete fool of yourself all over again.'

I resented her remarks. I felt trapped. Now I'd returned home to the nest, I wasn't to be allowed to try out my wings again.

I bought the *Singles* magazine, and mulled over the adverts in my room. There were pages of them. Mum kept sighing heavily, and tut-tutted in the way she does when she disapproves. Three in particular took my fancy, and I wondered if I dare answer them. I was still so unsure of myself, so insecure, and so lonely. Maybe others could go it alone, and would act differently given my set of circumstances. But I needed a special someone to love. I put pen to paper, and posted off my replies.

Box 2241 had been open, honest and direct:

> *Leftwing folksinger, 31, 5'5", seeks female singing partner with view to relationship. Voice unimportant, commitment vital. Car and house.*

I wrote in as light-hearted a manner as I could muster. I didn't want to sound inhibited or introspective. If we met, I meant to adopt a different approach, becoming a more alive and aggressive person.

Dear Advertiser,

A leftwing bachelor—I wonder what you mean by that? My main interest is music. I sing, play guitar and piano, as well as writing my own songs. I enjoy good company and good food, as well as drives in the countryside, although I must admit to not being able to drive myself. By the way, I note you don't say what your interests are. Perhaps you could give me some indication of some of these?

I am 25 next month, and five foot plus high. My hair is curly auburn, my figure curvy. Basically, it could be said I am a 'home-loving' bird, although I do have outside interests. I wonder what your likes and dislikes are?

I should be glad to exchange photos with you if and when you write . . .

I tried to take things as they came, and not to hope for too much. I found it depressing that my family were at a loss to understand my need for a man. They seemed to think this a cheap way of inviting trouble, and that I was in danger of getting caught on the rebound only to get hurt all over again.

1 July 1978
The reply came. Dad brought it up to me as I sat sipping my first cup of tea of the day, then hovered to see what it said.

Dear Janine,

Glad to get your letter, which has rather shaken my confidence in my ad. I didn't think I'd need to be more specific in describing myself as a leftwing bachelor! I'd be pleased to discuss this and many other matters, either on the phone, or preferably in person.

Briefly, I am also centrally involved with music. I've been a resident singer at the Grey Cock Folk Club since 1970, and I've gradually developed instrumental abilities over the years. I play guitar and dabble in several other instruments. I've also written a few songs.

Our circle of friends at the Grey Cock provides me with plenty of that 'good company' that I, like you, enjoy so much. Good food likewise, leading to dietary problems, but it's difficult to stop doing something as enjoyable as eating.

We organise regular weekend camping sessions at Talybont-on-Usk, which give us a chance to do ten mile hikes over the mountains, and provides great entertainment around the camp fire and in the pub. To that extent, I like the countryside! As for driving, I enjoy that greatly, thanks in no small part to my car which is a prized possession. It's a 1973 Porsche, a giant-killer with oodles of character.

In addition to finding these interests in common with you, I am also

*very fond of photography on a semi-professional basis, reading, games and
puzzles, Bridge, Chess, Scrabble, fringe theatre. I am also home-
loving (though I'm in a love-hate relationship with this one!)*

*If you are able and inclined, I'd much appreciate a phone-call today
between half-five and six, then we can arrange something. I can't find a
photo of me to enclose, but I'm short at 5'5", with ginger hair, and a
beard of small proportions. I'll take you as you come—what's inside is so
much more important!*

    All the best,
     Mike Turner

Red hair. I hoped he hadn't the temper to go with it. He sounded
nice, warm, genuine. My kind of man, with many interests and
talents. I had already made up my mind to follow this through, but
his final sentence clinched it. To know that what was inside me
mattered so much more than what I looked like gave me the
confidence I needed.

The moment I heard his voice on the phone, I knew this was it. I'd
tried to contain myself until just before six so as not to appear too
eager. Then my fingers had fumbled their way around the dial.
'Hello, is that Mike . . . Mike Turner?'

'Yes, Who's that?' His voice sent a shiver down my spine.

'Janine. You said to phone between half-five and six, and . . . ' I
was waffling, talking to cover my nerves.

'Hello, Janine.' He sounded cool and confident, yet at the same
time warm and friendly. I missed his next few words. I was too
busy dreaming up all the possibilities this encounter could bring. I
couldn't help myself. I'd missed too many opportunities in the past
to let this one pass me by. Now, I had built it up out of all
proportion. I knew I was hoping too hard, and I could get hurt.

'Would you like me to meet you somewhere for a drink and a
chat? Or maybe you'd prefer me to pick you up at your house?'

I opted for the latter, suddenly sensing a need within myself to meet
him on my home ground. Or maybe subconsciously, I was seeking
Mum and Dad's approval. They had been right about Bill, after all.

As I waited for him to arrive, strange feelings surged through my
body. Deep down, I felt a longing to be loved. My whole body cried
out for a man. I was pent-up, frustrated, moody, too ashamed of

what I was feeling to sit down and analyse my thoughts. I had always shied away from anything remotely connected with sex. To me, it was a dirty word. It meant Rape—and that hurt like hell. Yet, at the same time, I couldn't believe that true love and romance were really dead. I was confused, and a little frightened about the prospect of building up a relationship with another man. Yet strangely excited at the same time.

He breezed in, a busy, bustling body. 'I think we ought to sing,' he said, not wanting to waste time.

'I'll make some coffee,' I replied and I retreated hastily to the kitchen to plan my next move. It was all happening too fast. I hadn't had a moment even to catch my breath and assess him at close quarters. I knew the outfit I wore was quite wrong for the occasion, but it would look odd walking back into the room in something different. Besides, he had said in his letter that he would take me as I was.

I slipped back into the room to hear him playing my twelve-string guitar. He could play, I mean really play. When it was my turn, I found myself fumbling over my usual four-finger pluck. What was the matter with me? I had played in front of people before, so why did I feel inadequate now? I cut my performance short and, clutching the body of the instrument for comfort, tried to change the subject, 'I like your car.'

The purple Porsche sat solidly outside the window, its sleek lines gleaming under the street lamp.

'It's a 1973 model, a 911S, with a 2.4 litre engine . . . ' He was obviously an enthusiast. I tried to keep pace with the technicalities, interjecting an odd murmur of approval between sentences, while watching the way his face came alive as he warmed to his subject.

His hands rested neatly in his hip pockets, and he stood almost to attention as he talked, feet planted firmly on the floor. I wanted to reach out towards him, to feel his hand on mine, and to know that this was a man who would love me, and never let me go.

'Do you know much about cars?' His question held a challenge. Had I given away my secret desires by the expression on my face? Our eyes locked for a moment. Did I see the same kind of longing in him? For a fleeting moment, I thought I had, or maybe it was just something I wanted to see.

'No. I'm sorry. I hardly know anything about cars.'

He sat down suddenly. He was disappointed. I should have said before. 'Look, time's getting on. Shall I take you to a folk dance or something?'

I wondered if he was hastening the end of our meeting. I didn't want to share him with others. This might be the only time we had together, and I meant to treasure every moment. 'I'd rather go for a ride in your car.'

I excused myself on the pretext of getting a coat, and conversed with Mum and Dad in whispers at the top of the stairs.

'Doesn't he talk a lot! How is it going, Pet?'

'Oh, fine,' I murmured, trying to keep my voice light. 'We're going for a drive.'

'Oh, do you think you ought? I mean, you hardly know the man.'

A look of concern passed between my parents. Now was not the time to begin a heated discussion about letting their daughter make up her own mind.

I clattered down the stairs, and Mike joined me at the front door. Mum and Dad both came to see us off. I made the introductions, knowing they were giving him the once over.

'Don't wait up for me,' I flung over my shoulder. Then I put thoughts of them firmly out of my head as I set out to enjoy myself.

The evening had passed like a dream. We drove for some time in silence. I wondered if he'd noticed the gold band around my finger, and kept pulling at it as I tried to decide how to broach the subject. I wanted everything out in the open.

'I suppose you noticed my wedding ring?' I said, as my opening gambit.

'No . . . no I didn't.'

I detected surprise in his voice. Silence hung between us. Someone had to snap it.

'I'm separated. I'm divorcing my husband.' It sounded too formal, yet how could I begin? Where were the words that would sum it all up?

'I think I'd better take you to my place, and we'll talk it over there.'

119

We'd been travelling around in circles. Now Mike made a direct course for his home.

I was surprised to discover he lived in such a run-down area of Birmingham. I'd expected a palace compared to this. But home to him didn't mean home in the same way as it did to me. He was a bachelor, a freelance Computer Consultant, and as such, only needed a base in which to keep his belongings, and to come back to at night, or weekends if he was working away. It seemed an empty, lonely kind of life to me. No wonder he was advertising for a relationship.

We talked around the kind of qualities we looked for in other people, and I told him a little of my past life. He looked shocked. He was a gentleman—the kind of man who went ahead of a woman to open the door, pulled back seats for her to sit down. It was totally beyond his comprehension that someone could have treated me as Bill did. I warmed to him. He was a ready listener, easy to talk to. Yet I didn't want his sympathy. I didn't want him to feel sorry for me. I wanted, needed his love.

It was two in the morning when we drove back. We sat under the street lamp, ekeing out the evening, not wishing it to end. We'd still not touched, but for now it was enough to talk. It was a release to me, and I felt barriers coming down within me. I wanted to cling on, to cry out my love for this man. I began to believe in love at first sight because I was feeling it for myself.

Our goodbye was not a final one.

'I'll pick you up at seven tomorrow.'

'Tonight,' I whispered, smiling into the darkness. The curtains twitched at the upstairs window. I made for the front door, as the Porsche pulled away.

2 July 1978

Still sailing on Cloud Nine. Cannot yet get the wonderful evening and Mike, the man my heart has gone out to, off my mind. I am so lucky to have found someone like him, and I would be prepared to give my all if things keep on as they are. But is that enough, with all that he has to offer?

I feel already, that I have known him a lifetime. He feels for people, and doesn't just talk, but is prepared to act for what he believes in. It is incredible the number of interests he has: photography, folk music, trains, drama productions—none of which he plays around with or takes lightly. He has seen from experience what it is to love and be rejected, to give but receive nothing in return. I feel for him something which I cannot begin to describe. Is it love?

The hours till we met again stretched ahead interminably. I tried to fill them, sleeping late, then replaying the evening over and over again in my head. All I could think about was him.

That evening, he arrived as promised, and took me to his folk club. I tried not to mind sharing our time with others. I put on my social face, hid my inhibitions and shyness. He treated me as a friend, one of a crowd. His hand touched mine for only a moment as he reminded me of our pact to follow his special starvation diet. I sipped my single tomato juice, and concentrated on the words of the unfamiliar chorus I was trying to join in.

3 July 1978

I awoke feeling warm and vibrant all over. I felt like I had never done before. This had to be Love. I hugged myself, wishing they were his arms around me. We had sat under that same street lamp until almost three a.m. talking. Now I found it difficult to get up for my part-time cleaning job. I tried to keep busy, to fill my day with chores and shut out the thoughts of the evening ahead. It couldn't come soon enough.

He arrived as punctual as ever, and drove me to his house. But something was different. I felt frustrated, tense, knotted up inside. We sang a little, but the strain came through in my voice. He showed me breathing exercises to relax, and as he put his hands on my hips to demonstrate, a tremor ran down my spine. I half turned to throw my arms around him, I caught myself just in time. He moved away, and the moment passed.

Later we sat in silence. When at last we did speak, it was like some secret language of our own.

'You want it, don't you?' I dropped my eyes from the intensity of his gaze.

121

'Come on, admit it. Stop playing games.' I blushed. I wasn't being deliberately coy. I just had no idea of how to handle the situation.

'I don't know what you mean.' My pulse quickened. I was afraid of myself, of what I felt inside.

We bandied words for another ten minutes or so, before we finally reached a kind of decision.

'I will if you will.'

'All right then.'

We rose as one. I looked to him to lead, and in the hallway hung back, suddenly uncertain.

'Come on, I won't hurt you.'

Were they Bill's words, or Mike's? I pressed back against the wall, panicked. I wished I could shrink away out of sight.

He took my hand, and we nudged each other upstairs, a step at a time. We reached the bedroom. It was dark, but the bed was spotlit by the moon. I felt as if I were acting a part in a play. In a trance I removed my clothing, and when it lay in a crumpled heap on the floor, I folded up like a puppet with no-one to work my strings.

Mike was gentle, kind, considerate, everything a man should be to a woman. At first, it was difficult, painful, clumsy. We fingered, fidgeted, and fumbled through the overtures, but still our rhythm wasn't right. We kept falling out of step. Then, just as we thought we had it in our grasp, the phone rang. Our feeling of togetherness melted away. The spell was broken. That was it. I began to rise. But then we started afresh. Slowly, the feeling built up inside, carrying me on its crest, until it burst through like a spring out of the ground. It only lasted seconds, but to me it was the most beautiful moment imaginable. A single sound escaped my lips. A groan, a cry coming from deep down inside me. For the first time, I felt fulfilled.

There were no words to tell it how it was, yet I felt he understood. He had been there too? I climbed over the summit of the mountain on to the downward slope. I felt drained, tired, but with an almost suffocating awareness of ecstasy. I began to cry. I stared up at the ceiling, and felt as if I had waited years for that moment. It had triggered off something in me that craved for more. I wanted to be satisfied further. Once was not enough when I had waited so long.

Mike spoke, and with his words, I was thrown back into harsh reality. 'I'm sorry, Jan . . . but this isn't going to work.'

What was he saying? Hadn't we just been to heaven and back together?

'You're on your own. It was a joint decision that we do this, and I don't want any comeback. I don't want you to come crying to me if you're pregnant. You can't be that naïve that you didn't know what you were doing.' He kept hammering the point home.

On the way back in the car, he told me frankly what he felt, and why he didn't think there was any point in continuing our relationship.

'We can still be friends, can't we?' I asked, hesitantly. I couldn't bring myself to cut loose completely.

'Yes of course. Let me know how you're doing. Don't think I don't care simply because we're severing our ties.'

I had my own ideas as to why he was backing out suddenly. He seemed scared of the very thing he had been searching for for so long—a permanent, lasting love.

'You see, I have this kind of mental image of the kind of person I am looking for . . .' He was still trying to explain, to rationalise his fears. 'I have to experience this 'wow' feeling, so that I'll know that this is the person for me. I'm sorry, but I didn't feel that with you.'

I obviously didn't fit into his scheme of things, but it was hard to let go. There seemed nothing left to say. We stared at one another one last time under the street lamp, and then, crying inside, I said goodbye.

4 July 1978
My birthday, and I felt dead inside. How can life be so cruel?

I began to wonder if I had fallen for Mike simply because he was all the things Bill was not.

Two more *Singles* replies arrived—John '29-year-old professional bachelor'. Charles 'graduate recluse'. John's letter was facetious, full of puns. He would take my mind of Mike for a while.

He arrived outside the house in a sporty Lotus Europa. Had to bend his six-foot frame to get through the doorway, then stood hovering in the hall.

Outside, he took leggy strides towards the car. It was fur-lined, and I seemed to sink into my place in the front seat. I glanced at the driver and tried to think of something to say.

'I like the car.'

He had a set line to his lips which he tried to twitch into the trace of a smile as we roared off down the road.

He offered me a cigarette from a packet he produced from a concealed compartment in the dashboard. I shook my head. Smoke curled upwards from his own cigarette, and I tried not to cough. Blurred images leered at me from the past. Was this how life would be from now on, hopping hopefully from one man to the next, searching ever after for an elusive love that didn't exist?

We drew to a screaming halt in the car park of a club-house. John strode ahead, while I followed falteringly in his footsteps. We side-stepped tables laid for dinner and made for the bar.

He ordered a pint of bitter, and sat wrapped in his own thoughts for a time. I sipped a coke. Then suddenly he slammed down his glass and was off. It took me a moment to realise he was gone, and as I tried to slip elegantly off the stool, my skirt caught on the far side. I grappled with it, feeling my face flush. A man sitting next to me saw my difficulty, and reached over to unhook me. I scurried off after my partner like a frightened rabbit.

The car was roaring impatiently. I hardly had time to settle myself, before we hit the road, and took a bend too fast. We zigzagged in and out of a lay-by—I hardly dared blink in case I missed something—then screamed to a halt in the next parking place we came to. I glanced sideways, stiffening.

'How about it then?'

He took one look at my set expression, crashed the gears, and took off again at top speed. We made one more stop at a small country pub, where he left me at a table with a coke and strode off to talk to friends. Then we headed back.

It was still early as we parked outside the house.

'See you around.' He lit a cigarette and waited for me to go. His fingers drummed on the dashboard, and he looked irritably at his watch.

'I'm sorry I'm keeping you up.' I was angry, miserably disappointed, frustrated. I could have cried.

'Maybe I'll give you a ring sometime.'

I slammed the door hard. 'You needn't bother,' I muttered, and the car sped out of sight.

5 July 1978

'Graduate recluse' had arranged to spend the day with me, take me for a meal followed by a show. In many ways he sounded like Mike. His voice had been gently reassuring on the phone, and he described himself as 5'3", 31, with a beard and a moustache. He too worked with computers and I had high hopes for our meeting.

I opened the door to a small, nervous individual, who peered short-sightedly ahead. At his insistence we shook hands formally on the doorstep, before he stepped inside. There was an awkward silence once we were seated in the front room, coffee cups on our laps. A beard hid his face almost totally from view, and I tried not to copy his habit of bending forward to peer as I racked my brain for something to say.

'What would you like to do this afternoon?' We said the same thing simultaneously, and there was a moment or two of nervous laughter.

'Well, I wondered if you'd like to visit Aston Hall?' He was anxious. He wanted to please. His hand reached out hesitantly, and placed itself on mine. 'Please tell me what you would like to do? I'll take you for a meal afterwards, and we can get to know one another along the way.' I agreed I would like nothing better.

His tatty Morris Minor made a change after the cars I had been driven around in recently. But I was far from happy as we cruised carefully down the centre of the road, following the white lines. He sat hunched over the wheel, seemingly oblivious of angry hoots from other road-users.

He was a mild man by nature, totally incapable of a cross word. Anger was alien to him. Maybe that was one of the reasons I found myself warming to him. People pushed in front of us at Aston Hall, the guide left us behind, but Charles took me gently by the arm as if to show me off proudly as his prize.

It was a pleasant day, and I was made to feel like a queen. Nothing was too much trouble for him if it meant pleasing me. I began to think him the gentlest, kindest, most loving man imaginable.

Later in the cinema he whispered, 'You're the one for me.'

'But we've only just met,' I cautioned.

'I know, but I feel it here.' His hands reached for mine and placed them over his heart. It was a touching gesture, and I knew exactly what he meant.

He didn't need to explain. I felt the same way—about Mike. I had placed him high on a pedestal, just as this man was doing with me. Suddenly, I realised what it felt like. That was what had been wrong, what Mike had resented in our relationship. For a moment, however, I was tempted. Even if I didn't feel for Charles now in the same way as he did for me, I was sure these feelings could grow over the years. But memories of Mike held me back.

Much later we sat on the sofa in my parents' house, watching the late-night movie. Time ticked on until the white dot was all that was left of the screen. His arms wound round me. He was aroused, but somehow we had to say our goodbyes.

He was reluctant to leave. 'I'll call you later in the week, but promise me you will think seriously about what I have said?'

'I promise.'

It was no lie. I had a lot of hard thinking to do over the next few days.

At the front door he turned. I felt like a painting on display. I was about to speak, but he placed his finger over my lips.

'Let me remember you as you are, spotlit by the moon.' I watched him pulling on his driving gloves, very precisely pressing into place each finger in turn. Then he took one last lingering look at me and left. As his figure receded into the darkness, I caught a glimpse of how I could be in a couple of years—a bird in a gilded cage. I knew then that Charles was not for me.

9 July 1978

'Hello Mike, it's Janine.' My voice shook a little as I spoke.

'Hello.' He seemed surprised, and I didn't blame him. 'How are things going?' he continued.

I tried desperately to keep emotion out of my words. 'Well, I've lost half a stone,' I announced proudly.

'Really?' He was suitably impressed.

There was an awkward silence. I searched my mind for other news to stretch out the conversation. How could I begin?

'Mike . . .? Could you, I mean, would you take me with you to the folk club this evening?' I held my breath as I waited for his answer. I prayed selfishly as I used to as a child.

'Look, we agreed it was over. I'll give you instructions how to get there. But that's all.'

It was a start. I would work on it, and hope for more. He began to give me street names, bus times, and I muddled him with my poor knowledge of Birmingham. After some fifteen minutes or so, he sighed, 'I suppose you think I'm a pig as I've got a car, and could easily take you there myself?'

'Yes, I do,' I replied simply, unusually forthright. The battle was won.

The purple Porsche pulled up outside the house. I stood for one moment more in front of the mirror. If this evening was going to go the way I planned, I had to leave my feelings behind. Mum opened the door.

I fidgeted nervously with my skirt. Then calmly collected my coat from the rail. 'Coming?' I flung over my shoulder, and began walking towards the car. Mike caught me up, and I carefully kept my distance. I continued to keep the conversation light and inconsequential, my mind empty of thought.

Once at the club, I made for someone I had met last time, and stood talking, trying in some small way to prove my independence. Yet all the while, my eyes never left the bustling body, busily setting up tapes and mikes to record the singing. As I sat next to him, it was difficult to keep my hands to myself. I concentrated on the guest of the evening, and heartily joined in every chorus I could. I began to feel a part of it all, as if this was the family to which I belonged.

But the best part of all was when he drove me home. I told him about the other two men I had gone out with. He seemed genuinely

127

surprised—and pleased? He applauded my determination to carry on. We talked some more under the street lamp, and arranged a meeting the following night.

'Purely on the grounds of friendship,' he said, making it quite clear where we stood. I tried not to hope too hard as I crept up the stairs to bed.

10 July 1978

Mike seemed unusually unsure of himself. 'Look Jan, I have something to say, and it's hard . . .' I sat on the edge of the sofa, gripped the seat, and took a deep breath.

'I know I've treated you badly, and I'm sorry, but . . .' The 'but' hung between us for a long, long time before he spoke again. I tried to guess what it was he was going to say. Inwardly, I was preparing myself for the worst. I was sure this was the finale.

'I've been a fool, Jan. Forgive me. It's been staring me in the face all along, and I just couldn't see it. I was blind to my own emotions. Then, when I saw you the other night, I knew. Can we give ourselves another chance?'

I sat quite still, staring into space. His words seemed to float past me.

'Jan . . . do you hear? I'm asking for another chance. But I want to make it clear that I must be free to follow other opportunities if they should come along.'

I wished he hadn't added that final phrase. But I was determined to snatch even the smallest chance of happiness, so I ignored it. Hands reached out towards me, and we were locked in an embrace.

It was just like being young and in love for the first time all over again. The only black cloud was Mum and Dad's refusal to accept the situation.

Mike took the rest of the month to make up his mind finally, and I moved in with him shortly after. I became one of the folk club, and we went camping together. Days spent in domestication brought back a sense of belonging, and I revelled in the experience of being appreciated.

4 August 1978

We made beautiful music together. Harmonies floated back and forth. He was the words, I was the music, and he played me like an organ, pulling out all the stops so that my whole being vibrated. We reached that point when neither of us wanted it to end. The night was ours for the taking, and tomorrow just another day a long, long way away.

A loud, insistent knocking broke the spell. Someone was at the door. We tried to ignore it, but the world had intruded on our private place. We were no longer alone. We saw shadows pass the window, and I cautioned Mike to be careful.

'See what they want, but only open the door a crack. I have a funny feeling about this.'

My heart had begun to pound. Shivers ran down my spine. This was not a neighbourhood where night visitors were welcome. I padded cautiously to the window as Mike shut the door.

He was angry, 'Some stupid joker has tied a dog to the door-handle.'

I felt even more uneasy than I had before. I peered out into the darkness through a crack in the curtains. Just as I did so a brick crashed through the window, missing me by inches. It was a shock —a psychic shock—and I stood, shaking, as Mike rang for the police.

'It's OK Jan. Take it easy.'

I couldn't let go of the fear that this was Bill come for revenge. Somehow, he had sought me out. Would hound me for the rest of my days. I would never be free from the ghosts of my past.

I cowered in a corner, crying and ashamed. An overpowering sense of guilt carried me along on a wave of self-pity. It took a long time before I could face Mike again, let alone myself.

'I'm sorry, my love. I'm sorry,' was all I could sob.

The police arrived much later. There had been a spate of incidents in the area by a group of West Indians. The all-clear was sounded, and Mike made some tea. But I continued to cry. I couldn't rationalise my thoughts. Violence seemed as close to me here as it had ever been. Was there no escape?

Mum and Dad disagreed with my new way of life. It didn't seem to matter to them that I was healthier and happier than I had been in years.

'How could you do this?' they sighed. 'You're laying yourself wide open to get hurt all over again.'   .

Mum had a sad look back in her eyes and when we first walked down the garden to greet her, hand in hand, she simply turned away. She shut us out, putting up a barrier between us.

My divorce still hadn't come through and they couldn't accept another man in my life. I had broken my wedding vows, and put myself beyond the pale. Even my sisters were stand-offish. Meetings with my family became tense and strained. Everything they said seemed to be a leading question.

'How are things going then?' one of them would ask. I would interpret it to mean that if I answered anything less than perfect, it would prove them right about my having made another big mistake in my life. Maybe it was just me. Maybe I was being too sensitive, wanting to keep this new relationship special, and somehow secret. I tried to hide behind a face of indifference, masking the hurt I felt inside. I had admitted my former marriage was a mistake—surely I didn't have to pay for it for the rest of my life.

I felt so emotionally drained, so on edge in their company that I became glad when the ordeal was over. I couldn't find words enough to explain. If they couldn't see my happiness, my acceptance of Mike, what hope had I of their consent, of their being happy because I was happy?

18 August 1978
People talked trivia around us. We tried to join in, to become part of the crowd. It was a tea-party organised by Mum and Dad, but with their friends not ours. We knew no-one. I turned to the lady on my left, and made a passing remark about the weather. Before I had finished speaking, she turned away, and made motions to someone behind. Mike appeared to be having a similar breakdown in communications.

I leaned forward towards a tray of food, and on impulse, deliberately upset a plate of neatly arranged sandwiches. It seemed to be the signal between us for suppressed feelings to be released. We sent cakes, puddings, and pies flying in all directions. Once begun, we couldn't stop. At first the people gathered around us sat still, stunned and surprised. Then, as they realised what we were doing, they seemed shocked, upset, and angry. Tables turned, cloths were stained brown with tea, plates smashed, chairs fell over. When everything lay in a mess about us, we ran off.

A bedroom. A figure entered, uninvited, and the couple on the bed parted. Mike made for the window, and dropped into the alley below. Mum gave chase, and I followed in their wake, afraid of what the outcome might be. We all three clattered through a maze of corridors. Mum was gaining on Mike, then I lost sight of them as they rounded the final corner. My breath was coming in short gasps and my legs almost gave under me, but I forced them on . . . and on . . . and on.

Mum stood alone. Mike had disappeared.

'What have you done with him?' I screamed, as I saw the axe in her hands. She smiled back contemptuously.

'Mike, Mike my love,' I called into empty space.

I awoke, sweating, confused. Comforting arms hugged me to him until I knew I was safe.

'No-one will take me from you.' Mike talked softly, silencing my fears. 'I promise my darling, I will never leave you.'

The same dream came back again and again.

23 August 1978

Met family in town today for salad lunch. I felt so emotionally withdrawn and restricted in their company, that I was quite relieved when I left. I feel as though I am somehow in the wrong all the time. I feel so guilty, that I can hardly speak face to face with any of them. Is it me, or them? Why do I feel this way when they are my own family? It can't be normal.

I feel I am being pressured, being made to account for my actions. I continually withdraw from the conversation because I feel so inadequate, inhibited, inferior. I choose my words carefully, and then wait on tenterhooks to see how they are received. Am I supersensitive?

It is almost as if they believe I have passed the point of redemption. Every new thing I say I am becoming involved in just seems to add to the feeling against me, and confirms in their eyes, that I am putting my own morals and beliefs to the back of my mind. As if I am doing what I do simply to please Mike.

Christmas Day 1978
Mike proposed!

We'd been busy with presents all morning, and then taken our time tucking into a huge turkey. It wasn't until the evening, when we turned off the television to enjoy simply being together, that we found the words.

'If your decree absolute is confirmed as expected on the 16th of next month, we could be married by special licence on the 18th.'

Not the most romantic of proposals, but it meant the world to me. I savoured the moment, rolling it round in my mind. Then I felt an overwhelming desire to share my happiness with Mum and Dad.

'Hello. Happy Christmas everyone,' I almost shouted down the phone with excitement. Then I found myself holding back, keeping the news at bay. I couldn't find a way to tell them. I wasn't sure how they would take it.

'Are you all having a good time?' Such a trite remark, when what I wanted to say was so much more important. 'And what did you get in your stockings?'

Still I'd found the words wouldn't come. They stuck in my throat. Each time I'd tried to say them, something else came out instead.

'I love you. We wish we could be with you.' We were coming to the end of the conversation. Goodbyes were already being said.

'Mum . . ?'

'Yes . . ?' It came between us like a barrier.

'Mum . . ?' I began again. Mike's hand found mine, as I said in a rush, 'I've just been proposed to, and I'm so deliriously happy.' I held my breath, then let it out to add in a small quiet voice, 'Please, please be happy with me.'

The telephone line crackled as I waited for her to reply. I wanted to see her face, to throw my arms around her, to let her know everything was wonderfully all right. Yet at the same time I was thankful to have space between us.

'And did you accept?' I almost missed her words.

'Of course I did,' I said, indignantly.

Hushed, hurried whispers at the other end, then Dad came on the phone, 'Well we'll leave it at that for now, poppet. We'll be in touch again soon.'

Their obvious lack of enthusiasm left me feeling flat and disappointed. We drank a toast to each other from a bottle of Bristol Cream in an attempt to put the sparkle back into Christmas.

Later, I discovered my parents had been very upset at the news. It had evidently come as a shock, and yet our love had been there, plain for all to see. But they'd remembered my first engagement, and how I'd displayed my ring proudly without a word of warning at Christmas 1973. They were taking it the same way now as they had done then. It crucified me inside to think that they didn't understand how different things were this time.

1979

Advice is what we ask for when we already know the answer but wish we didn't.

ERICA JONG

17 January 1979

It was somehow fitting that the date of my second marriage should be 18 January 1979. My marriage to Bill had been on 19 January 1974. One seemed to cancel out the other.

At the courts on the eve of our wedding we were given a cool welcome by the receptionist on duty.

'Good morning. Can I help you?' she said formally, with not even the hint of a smile. To her we were just another couple.

But this was a big moment for me. I wanted a clash of cymbals to signal the end of an era, a bugler to herald my new beginning. It was the end of oppression, and the start of a new kind of freedom. I had been granted my Decree Nisi, and now I needed a Decree Absolute to dissolve my marriage completely. I wished it was as easy to blank out the past, and begin again, free from the nightmares that still shadowed my new-found happiness.

'Ah yes, Mrs. D— You'll have to wait a few minutes. There's been a mistake . . .' The lady behind the desk looked a little less self-assured.

'A mistake?' My first thought was that Bill had chosen to contest at the last moment.

The receptionist disappeared behind a partition for what seemed an eternity, then came back carrying a sheaf of forms. I clutched the desk for support, preparing for the worst.

'I'm afraid this is going to take time.' She was prolonging my

134

agony. I screamed loud and long inside my head.

'We have a few forms for you to fill in.' She indicated with a stab of her finger where I should sign. 'Now sections A, B, C, D, are correct. But we need you to fill in the missing details on C.'

I obliged, still expecting her to say at any moment that Bill was demanding me back.

'Right, that's about it I think.' She brought down the stamp of officialdom, and handed me my papers. With a 'next please' I was free to go.

I WAS FREE!

18 January 1979

The registry office was like a doctor's waiting room. We sat, huddled together, listening for our names to be called. I felt as if I were drugged or drunk, walking around in a dream, my divorce papers clutched to me. My passport to freedom. I couldn't believe it was happening. It was my happy-ever-after ending coming true. Then we were being led into the inner sanctum, to be clinically dealt with by the immaculately dressed man in charge. We answered the questions he put to us in hushed, nervous whispers, overawed by our surroundings.

'Janine, will you take Michael Laurence Joseph Turner to be your lawful wedded husband? Will you love him, comfort him, honour and keep him in sickness and in health, as long as you both shall live?'

The man's voice droned on. It sounded bored, as if he had said the same words too many times before. It was a solemn moment, but I wished he could have looked more alive, put some feeling into the proceedings. He stood stiff and formal, waiting for my reply. A lady sat at his side, pen poised, ready to ink in the details, to put the final seal of approval on our marriage.

I felt for Mike's hand, and slipped mine into his. I wondered what he was thinking.

'I look like a monkey in a suit, sticking out in all the wrong places,' he'd said, when we'd gone to buy new clothes for the occasion. 'And I'll be so nervous, you'll be able to hear my teeth chatter.'

He hadn't looked forward to being the centre of attention. Yet, standing next to him now, I felt so proud.

I fiddled with the emerald engagement ring, and smoothed out an imaginary crease in my green velvet suit. I wished it were a white wedding dress with a long lace train, that this were a church not an office. No bridesmaids, no bells ringing, not even a bouquet. And where were the people—my parents, Mike's mother, our aunts and uncles, relatives and friends? I cast my thoughts aside. It didn't matter. Only the love and happiness I felt within mattered.

Now, in the small ceremony that was taking place, I finally spoke the words everyone was waiting to hear:

'I will,' I said, clearly and distinctly.

We were man and wife—Mr and Mrs Michael Turner.

'Too late to back out now,' Mike's brother kidded as we traipsed out in single file.

'When are we going to eat?' The children were restless, and hungry.

We posed for a photo or two on the steps, while the world walked uncaringly by. It was a blustery January day, and I pulled up my collar against the cold.

24 January 1979
After a few days of marriage, I found that that little piece of paper called a marriage certificate hadn't made any difference. I still had the dreams, the guilt and everything else that went with them. We had many problems to overcome and decided to seek professional help. We prepared ourselves for our first session with the analyst by playing word association.

'Day,' I began.

'Night,' replied Mike, logical as ever.

'Black,' I countered.

'White.'

'Pain,' My voice dropped to a whisper.

'Pain?' queried Mike.

'Pain.'

'Hurt,' Mike continued.

'Bruised.' Again, my words were whispered, and I found I was crying. It wasn't a game any more, it was reality. My life started to pass before me as Mike tried to change the subject. Every word we began with thereafter, ended the same way. We needed help.

27 January 1979
The first session was spent more or less getting to know one another. Neither of us expected the quietly spoken man who greeted us at the door of a very striking house, and led us into a study. We each sat in comfortable armchairs while he sat on a cushioned couch. He sat quietly, content to listen while we talked. Well, Mike mostly. I remained in the background slightly overawed by it all.

We outlined our 'symptoms' such as in my case: dreams; saying sorry; wanting to please; suppressed anger; inability to talk openly, to swear, or to say certain words connected with sex. Mike's were slightly more surface things such as becoming technical as a cover for shyness and embarrassment; switching off and going into a world of his own while his thoughts went through a computer-like programme, triggered off by some chance remark.

The session seemed to last only about half an hour, when in fact we went well over our time. Next time he wanted to see just me, as I seemed the more urgent perhaps. He would come back to Mike at a later date.

3 February 1979
We arrived at this second session prepared for just me going in, but in fact both of us were needed initially to give details of dates of birth, address, etc. He decided to see us both one after the other in future on Saturdays, and for me to attend on Tuesdays as well. Mike went off into the next room, while I spouted on about childhood.

I talked at length about the sheltered atmosphere in which I was brought up, centred around the Church and all the good things in life. It was a happy time, yes—but also I had wondered whether there wasn't more to life, more to see and learn. Mum and Dad

137

seemed reluctant to let me and my sisters loose in the cruel, bitter world. They seemed to live within their own private world, letting no bad or evil penetrate, and wanting us to see only the good in people. We were not prepared for what was to come. They loved us too much to let us learn by experience, and seemed to think we had already learned all that there was to know. They wanted to protect us, wrap us in cottonwool, and they believed in the Church and the Family Unit above all else. Ideally, I was sure they would have welcomed the chance to have us move only as far as next door to them, if we had to move at all. Twenty-eight or thirty was the age at which they expected us to marry, and then into a good, Christian family.

The session stopped as I reached the age of eight. But later, when Mike and I were going over what had been said, I realised how much I had missed out. I had only mentioned the visits to hospital in passing, and also the fact that I had had to wear hospital shoes for a long time. But I said nothing about the calipers, the green railings, and the white-coated figures I grew to fear and hate, the figures which are still usually uppermost in my mind at the mention of hospital.

6 February 1979

I experienced initial nerves as if I were going to the dentist, but perhaps they were due to my making the journey on my own. In any case there were no problems to worry about. I arrived early, but could begin straightaway. This time I felt more able to talk about the past as it really was.

The word around which this session seemed to be centred was 'different'. I talked at length about how I was different from other children with my calipers, and how each time we moved I dreaded having to make friends again and explain about my foot. Then I left school, only to have to restart in order to be able to study music to 'A'-level standard. There I was different again, because people in my class were two years younger than I was. I felt a failure, and that I had let Mum and Dad down, when I didn't get either R.E. or Music 'A'-level. This feeling continued when I married Bill against their wishes and it didn't work out. I had wanted to go to College instead of going back to school which I hated, and this is the only thing I regret not having done because I lacked the courage at that time to stand up against my parents.

The rest of the session was spent talking about my marriage to Bill. How I spent my life waiting on or for him, and refused to let rip enough to strike him back as everyone told me I should. Once again I was different. I expected to be hit, abused and walked over, and to have as little money as possible. It was the norm. Then there was Kate and all the trouble that followed that.

The analyst commented on how empty of feeling I was about the events, and how I had managed a kind of transference of the anger *I* should have been feeling into him, the same way as I did with Mike. But he seemed to think that some of my barriers stemmed from childhood, and were only brought out during my marriage to Bill. He also pointed out that instead of thinking myself a failure, I should think perhaps about how my parents had failed me in some respects.

10 February 1979

Third session left me feeling that at last we were getting somewhere. It was more about my emotions and how I felt, rather than a history of events. We went back to that bedroom in that council house and I remembered so vividly the empty feeling I had there, of being totally alone and rejected. I talked about the book I was reading and how I identified with the heroine, a little innocent, who was never prepared for womanhood or for how cruel and evil the world can be. The analyst called me simple and childlike in my ways and in how I looked at life, and asked me if I felt that way about myself. I remembered that it had been a shock when I found out that the world wasn't such a big, beautiful place as I'd imagined, but after that I just accepted everything that came along. 'Good attracts evil,' he mused. Then I related the experience of being kissed for the first time and of spending the next six months in apprehension, thinking I was pregnant. I had even imagined that I was growing, then that I had felt the baby move. I was scared rigid.

We talked for a long time about how Mike and I had met, the climax of my plan to beat my depression, but I was shy of saying too much on this subject. Somehow I felt as if I had to justify my actions—to the analyst or to myself, I don't know. I kept saying how lucky I realised I was, having lived and experienced. The people I went out with before Mike and I got back together seemed so empty. Even though I had been stuck in a rotting marriage for four and a half years, I had seen more of life than any of them, and had got a lot more out of my existence so far. I felt that perhaps I wasn't so wasted and downtrodden after all. I had a lot to be proud of after scraping myself off the floor and making something of myself before it was too late.

Also in this session we talked of how my role throughout my marriage to Bill was similar to that of the mother of a wayward child. Just as I had experienced withdrawal symptoms after my phantom pregnancy, I now seemed to be having the same feelings, as if I had lost a child to look after and needed a replacement. The analyst seemed to think this was very evident. Even Bill when he did admit occasionally he had done wrong, did so like a naughty child who expects to be punished or at least reprimanded.

13 February 1979

I began this session by describing the three strange episodes I experienced over the weekend. The first took place in the kitchen— I swung round surprised at an imaginary child's voice saying 'Mummy'. The next incident took place while I was still in bed on Sunday morning and Mike had gone out to get some milk. The wind must have made the bedroom door open a little, then I heard the same child's voice saying that it wanted a cuddle and to give Daddy a surprise when he came back by hiding under the bedclothes. The final mysterious episode occurred on Sunday night as we were going out to the folk club. It was more of a conversation that took place this time. I was telling the child that Mummy and Daddy were going out, and it had to be good for Aunty. In each instance I saw the child, never knowing if it was a boy or a girl, but with a beautiful head of curls. So real, yet all in my imagination.

I went on to relate how Sunday evening had been our first public attempt at singing together. While singing one of my songs, *'April '78'* I had felt all the feelings that I should feel when I talked about the past welling up inside me and at the finish I was hard pushed not to cry. The analyst commented that I seemed to have got used to hiding my emotions below the surface, and this triggered off memories of my guilt at not being able to show my love for Mum any more by way of hugs, kisses, or terms of endearment. After I stopped saying prayers with her at night, I seemed to close in on myself. Since then I have had the impression that she thinks I have lowered my standards.

I made it clear at the end of the session that I do not condone or criticise any of my parents' actions. I was simply retelling the incidents as I saw them. I love them both very dearly. In reply to the analyst's question about whether I had ever told my parents to shut up, or stood up for myself against them even more forcibly, I said that I had never openly rebelled—unless my marriage to Bill could be termed as rebellion. I had at all times put their feelings first, and even put aside what I had to do for fear of hurting them. When I tried to leave Bill earlier I remembered asking myself what my parents would think. And yet it was my life.

17 February 1979

I was very disappointed and depressed with this session, mainly because I went into it with the feeling of something specific having been achieved, and I thought we were getting somewhere at last. But he sat in his usual chair in his usual way, with an aloof and indifferent expression, while I tried to recount what had happened at home.

I had been very moved by a TV programme about a young widow who, after her husband's tragic death, had remade her life with her young son. Her life appeared to run on a parallel course with my own life. At first she lived like a hermit, preferring her own company to that of others, and refusing to answer the door to callers. Then she changed her life by joining in the activities of her local Community Centre. She met a young man while out shopping one day. One thing led to another. They married and now she was pregnant.

I related to the analyst how this programme had seemed to trigger off a chain-reaction, and how shortly afterwards I was feeling all the pent-up pain I was trying so hard to ignore. Mike and

I had talked it out on his return from work, and suddenly three separate accounts of happenings that took place in the dark began to force their way out. Once begun I couldn't stop, but strangely when I did stop eventually, I couldn't remember them at all. I didn't remember anything until I went through it all again with the analyst. In all this time he didn't say a word, and he didn't reply when I asked whether he wanted me to carry on.

It was a syrupy, gooey darkness, sweet like tea. I had a cup by the side of me which someone was trying to force on me. Mist turning to grey then white. But I just wanted to sleep, to be left alone . . .

The other two darkness episodes escaped me during that session—perhaps because I didn't want to remember. The session ended and I felt I had lost out somewhere along the line. I asked the analyst whether he thought the episodes as important as we did, but he evaded the question. He didn't bring it up with Mike, even though I told him Mike had notes on what had happened. I was hurt and frustrated by his lack of help. I needed to know what my subconscious refused to let through.

Much later I was able with Mike's help to relive the other two darkness incidents. We felt them to be of the utmost importance, especially since I have been unable to feel or cry properly since I left Bill.

In bed in dark. I awake to find a hand moving over me. I instinctively move to my side of the bed. Movement becomes more urgent, grabs, becomes insistent that I pay heed to its demands. I feel pressured, stifled. I push it away. Hand becomes cruel. Pinches nipples painfully. Moves further down. Great pain in lower regions— no, not wet. Nails bite in. Hurts but I know that if I cry out the hand will either clamp itself over my mouth, or else slap me. I can feel every move it makes. Weighed down, then more pain as he moves on top. Dominant. I cry out and there is a pause. 'Well, you'll do it anyway. It's about time.' All the time darkness, and the furtive movements of the hand. Now impatient. 'Not again . . . please!' 'Yes, you'd better do it this time.' Thrusts. Not wet. I cringe. Cry out why is it always the same? Thrusts again because it will not go in. In, out, in, out. 'Why can't you be like other women?' Let it be over soon. I'm a failure, I know, so why not leave me in peace? No good as a woman, no good as a wife. Cannot keep my man happy. Then it is over and I am left to cry quietly, softly so as not to wake him, or he will send me into the cold spare room for the remainder of the night. Left with the feeling that it's all my fault.

The third darkness episode is, in my belief, myself, coming round after having been knocked out.

From dark comes grey. Then gradually I become aware of pain all over, but particularly my head. Not just aching, hurting. I feel bumps. I find I am lying on the floor by the side of the bed. I feel terrible. I cannot think straight. My mind goes blank when I try to think back over the last few hours. All I can think of is the dinner to be cooked, washing-up to do, rooms to tidy, beds to make. I try to stand up, but my legs are wobbly. Each turn of my head brings new pain.

20 February 1979

My final session with the analyst. After Saturday's session had left me so upended and depressed, Mike and I decided that, due to our close relationship and total involvement with one another, we seemed to be doing more for ourselves on our own. The analyst spent the whole of our time just sitting back and letting us talk, only raising an eyebrow questioningly if we stopped, then at the end he called 'time' and prepared for our next meeting. He did drop one or two words now and again, more as 'prompters' than anything else. He offered no words of sympathy or advice.

On arrival at this session I handed him a typed letter, but he refused to read it until I had had my say. I explained that on Saturday I had felt inhibited by the fact that I had not had any encouragement or comeback from him, and had left in a very confused and frustrated state. I had felt angry with him for not helping me and for not having discussed the darkness episodes with Mike even though I had asked him to. I had also felt angry with myself for not having been able to be more forthcoming. I was disappointed that these episodes which to me had seemed such a good thing to happen, had been glossed over by him and in no way taken up. He replied that I, or we, were expecting too much. He would need lots more time for any results to be seen, and I got the impression that it would all have been conducted along similar lines—us spouting and him listening. I thought that we needed more guidance, but we could not hope to get it from someone like him who wouldn't even hint at any progress having been made, and made no comment on anything we said.

However, we parted on a friendly note, and he did say that should we wish to continue at some time in the future, we had just to phone. I still like to think that he helped a little—and who knows whether he did in fact set off the process that resulted in the episodes, or whether we instigated that ourselves by our intense analytical sessions at home.

The whole thing cost us £100.

24 February 1979
Another episode. We had gone to bed early and I had just laid aside my magazine in preparation for going to sleep, when a noise at the door made me jump, and then there I was back in that large empty bed in ——. There I had woken to a similar noise and had lain trying to convince myself that it was all in my imagination.

The noise came again distinct in the darkness. I froze. The darkness seemed to close in on me, smothering, suffocating. Yet I couldn't move. My body was paralysed with fear. The next thing I remember is the hand groping in the darkness. Warm breath and the heat of another body close to mine. Then contact. Panic as the hand gripped, twisted, hurt. Thrusting until my insides felt as if they were being torn apart. My mind became alive with pain. I couldn't think, only feel and hurt. I screamed and writhed, trying my hardest to avoid the hand over my mouth. I was in agony, not knowing when it would end.

It was Bill. He hadn't gone to work, but had gone to the pub instead, and had returned home drunk. He had stumbled about in the darkness, then later come to bed lusting for action.

Much, much later I recalled the sequel. I had gone to sleep with the light on, and had woken to see the door handle moving backwards and forwards. Terror gripped me again, but I was determined to overcome it. I closed my eyes in an effort to compose myself, only to open them again a few seconds later. I burst out crying with relief—Bill stood in the doorway. One of his sick practical jokes.

After this episode Mike and I went over it and talked it out, but this time we had no analyst present. We remained convinced that we were making more progress on our own.

1983

To every thing there is a season, and a time to every purpose under the heaven: a time to be born, and a time to die; . . . a time to kill, and a time to heal; a time to break down, and a time to build up; a time to weep, and a time to laugh; a time to mourn, and a time to dance; . . . a time to keep, and a time to cast away; . . .

ECCLESIASTES, Chapter 3, Verses 1-6

The evil sorcerer and wicked witch are now safely locked in my past. I threw away the key long ago. Yet their ghosts still haunt me. They still cast a shadow of despondency over today, intrude on the present, mar my otherwise perfect existence. The nightmares live on, and I wonder if I shall ever be free.

Little is said about the inner barriers that grow in a bad marriage. Mine were built up over a period of five years. Who knows how long they will take to break down? My self-confidence had been chiselled away into almost nothing. It is only now, with Mike's help, that I am learning to come to terms with myself as a person in my own right. Somehow, I feel as if I left a part of myself behind when I uprooted myself from my past. Since the day I left, I have never shown anger, or said a cross word. I still tend to tense up, and duck out of the way of the expected blow, if Mike so much as raises his voice. I dread meeting people, and sometimes wake screaming in the night, after a nightmare about beatings, fear, and rape.

I used to resent my past coming between us like this. Now I accept it, because it is a part of me. Without it, I wouldn't be able to appreciate today. I cannot blank it out, or pretend it didn't

146

happen. Even now it only takes the slightest thing to trigger off all the old reactions which reduce me to a shaking wreck. For instance, just the other day, Mike was working late in his study. He had a technical problem to cope with on the computer, and was feeling a strain.

'Come to bed, love. Leave it until morning.' I disturbed his train of thought.

'Not now,' he snapped. 'Leave me alone.'

'I'll make some coffee.' I lingered in the doorway, loving him, unwilling to leave.

'Go away, Jan. Can't you see I'm busy.'

I ran away to the farthest corner of the house, and cowered down, head in hands. I hurt as if I had been dealt a physical blow. I was tense, rigid with fear, my face twitching with fright. It took Mike another half hour or so to coax me back. Even then, I felt insecure, unsure. It happens all the time. My past is part of me and will still on occasion not be denied.

Helping obliterate that past is my daughter, Joanne, who clamours for attention.

'Mummy . . . mummy . . . mummy . . .' she murmurs, almost to herself. Then she screams excitedly as I chase her around the room. I push my diaries aside, putting the past behind me for the moment, and stoop to pick her up.

It took a year of false hopes, a series of tests, and an operation to remove the physical scars that Bill had left inside me, before the way was clear for our baby to be born. Now, at two-and-a-half, she is the missing piece of the puzzle, put firmly into place. My picture is complete. I am fulfilled.

Appendices

The following interviews with representatives of the DHSS, the legal profession, the caring professions, and Women's Aid are intended to show how a battered woman is likely to be treated today, if she were to approach any of these agencies. It is to be hoped that any woman in this situation will find as much sympathy and concern as the author was shown by the representative selection she approached. The publishers would like to thank them for giving so much of their time.

DHSS
(interviewed 6 June 1983)

Author: What does the DHSS understand by the term 'separated'?

DHSS: By that term we understand a married couple to have parted, to be living apart from one another. Simply that. The marriage is disrupted.

Author: Then do you class a battered wife simply as a separated wife with additional problems?

DHSS: Well yes, if she is in fact living apart from her husband. As you know, there are many battered wives who continue to live with their husbands. It is the fact of separation, rather than the fact that a woman is a battered wife that we would be considering.

Author: What help then can the DHSS give a battered wife who has left her husband on the grounds of cruelty?

DHSS: Here again we are talking about a wife who is living apart from her husband and the reason given for the separation is the fact that she has been assaulted. If the woman comes into the office and makes a claim, then we will take a claim for Supplementary Benefit to which she would probably be entitled. We will speak to her about the other Benefits to which she might be entitled. Entitlement to some of the Benefits depends on a variety of factors e.g. are there children?

If we take the case of a woman without children, there would of course be no entitlement to Child Benefit. If, however, the woman has been in regular full-time employment, there might be entitlement to a Contributory Benefit. But if there is no contributory record then inevitably we are speaking about Supplementary Benefit. This is a means-tested benefit and certain conditions must be met. For example, Supplementary Benefit cannot be paid to a person who has available assets of more than £2,500.* (*£3,000 from November 1983.) However, if a woman satisfies the conditions, then we will award an allowance to meet her particular requirements.

Following what I said earlier, where there are children in the case of the woman, Child Benefit will be payable. In addition and because the woman is now effectively a lone parent, the One Parent Benefit could then become payable when the separation has lasted for thirteen weeks. I should add that these two benefits are taken into account in the calculation of Supplementary Benefit.

It may be, however, that the woman is still in full-time employment in which case there will be no entitlement to Supplementary Benefit. Child Benefit and One-Parent would still be payable, provided there were children in her care and additionally Family Income Supplement could be claimed.

You now begin to realise the variety of Benefits which are available to a wife who is separated from her husband.

Author: Would you give the woman any advice regarding legal action for example?

DHSS: We would certainly explain the Legal Aid scheme and, if she requested it, we would give her the address of a Legal Aid solicitor. The giving of legal advice is for the legal profession and not for my Department, though clearly we would have some interest in the outcome of her interview with the solicitor.

Author: Will she get a sympathetic hearing if she goes into a busy DHSS office, finds herself in an enormous queue, gets up to the counter and says she is a battered wife who has left her husband? Will she be dealt with in the queue at that point?

DHSS: Well, no. For everybody's sake it would be best for her to make an appointment beforehand. It is a big, big step for a woman to leave her husband and I think she would be unlikely to go into a DHSS immediately after the separation. I think she would probably sit down first and consider her position, including the fact that she will require an income. My advice to her is to phone the local DHSS office and make an appointment beforehand. Then there is no need to stand in a long queue. When she keeps her appointment, her name will be called and she will be shown into an interview room. If the interview has to be completely private, then we do have private rooms in most of our more modern offices. Long queues do not occur so often now in any case, since we have gone over to the appointments system. But yes the woman would be dealt with sympathetically, as the officer dealing with her case would be aware that as a battered wife she has special problems.

Author: When she phoned would she have to ask for a special kind of DHSS officer, or should she simply phone her local office and explain what she required to the person who answered the phone?

DHSS: Well, if she simply told the person on the switchboard that she was a separated wife, that person would then be able to direct her to the division that would deal with her case. The person on the switchboard would ask for her name and the woman would be directed to the section of the office that deals with that part of the alphabet. A lot of offices, although not all, use this system, but, whatever the system, the receptionist would be able to direct her.

Author: I understand that the DHSS does have some kind of emergency set-up, if the woman was desperate, so that she could get money very quickly?

DHSS: Yes, if her need is immediate, then it is possible to issue a Giro over the counter there and then to meet this need. Normally, however, these things are dealt with by post. We would aim to get a Giro out to her on the day that she was interviewed, so that she would receive it the following day. That's the general aim of the organisation.

Author: Will the DHSS help her to support herself if she is staying with family or friends?

DHSS: Certainly. The rates of Supplementary Benefit vary according to the claimant's circumstances. For instance, if we take two examples: a person will be classed either as a householder or a non-householder. Now you mentioned if she is living with friends or relatives. By our definition she is then a non-householder and would be paid the rate of benefit which is payable to a non-householder of whatever age. If she is a householder and still paying the household expenses, then the amount of Supplementary Benefit payable would be higher.

Author: Will the DHSS help her if she leaves her husband to live with another man?

DHSS: The answer is no. Generally speaking, when a woman is living with another man who is not her husband, she is required to look to that other man for her maintenance. The Supplementary Benefit Act provides that where a couple live together, whether they are legally married or not, their resources are aggregated as are their requirements and claims have to be made by the man of the couple. However, the rules are being changed in November of this year and at that stage, although we don't know the details of it yet, there will be circumstances in which the woman will be able to claim for the man with whom she is living, and for any children that there are. Equality of opportunity is what it comes down to.

Author: Will a part-time job affect her claim?

DHSS: Indeed yes. We can ignore part of a part-time job's earnings. Anyone in full-time work is totally excluded from receiving Supplementary Benefit, so it's got to be part-time work for Supplementary Benefit to be paid. But what we can do for a single parent is to disregard the first £4 of any earnings plus half the balance up to £20, so for a woman with children who's earning £20 in a part-time job, we can ignore £12 of those earnings and take £8 into account. So the answer is yes, a part-time job can very well affect the amount of Supplementary Benefit that becomes payable. Where the woman has no children, only £4 of the net earnings can be ignored.

Author: What about proof? Does the woman have to prove to you that she is a battered wife, or does she have to prove simply that she has left her husband?

DHSS: Well, the battered wife aspect is, to some extent, incidental to the main reason for the claim. We are dealing, as I said earlier, with a separated wife i.e. a wife who has left her husband, or who has been deserted by her husband. The history of assaults is the reason for the separation. The evidence that we would be looking for is evidence that she is in fact living apart from her husband.

Author: Would the DHSS keep her whereabouts secret from her husband?

DHSS: In the general case of a separated wife that is seldom necessary. The husband's solicitor has in fact a right to know where the wife is living. But in a battered wife case, yes, we would keep her address secret from her husband.

Author: What about maintenance? Will the DHSS pursue the husband if he refuses to pay maintenance?

DHSS: We generally encourage the woman to raise her own Action. It's to her advantage when the Action is finally obtained to have the Court Order in her own name, because at any time from then on she is able to enforce her own Court Order for maintenance. Now, it is the case, when a woman is reluctant, or unable, or unwilling to raise her own Action, that we as a department can raise an Action for maintenance against the husband for the wife and for children from whom he is separated, but I stress that that order is then in favour of the DHSS. We would certainly continue to pay the woman Supplementary Benefit, if that's what she was entitled to, but if that woman ceases to receive Supplementary Benefit at some time, perhaps if she starts full-time employment, she has no Court Order in her own name. We still have the Court Order which we obtained when we raised the Action. This is why we try to encourage women to raise their own Actions and obtain their own Court Orders.

Author: I have heard that there exists in Scotland something commonly known as a 'bed and board' law. Do you know what is meant by this?

DHSS: It means that a husband has an obligation to entertain his wife at bed and board i.e. to give his wife a roof over her head, to provide for her needs and to feed her. In this context I think care has to be exercised when dealing with the case of a wife who leaves her husband unreasonably. Now if a wife leaves her husband and tries to pursue him for maintenance, and he says that his door remains open to her, then in Scotland the woman may not have legal grounds for remaining apart from him. The reason for the separation becomes most important and it is quite conceivable that the Court might find that the husband is not liable to maintain that wife while she remains away from him. The Court may take the view, since the man has offered to give his wife a home, that he has met his legal obligations.

Author: But if she did continue to live apart from her husband, given that the Court took that view, would the DHSS still help her?

DHSS: Yes. We would not wish to become deeply involved in legal arguments between the husband and the wife, if the Court has decided that the wife has no good reason for staying away from her husband. We are always reluctant to get into a position, for example, where the husband can accuse us of encouraging his wife to stay away from him in defiance of the law. Our obligation is not to resolve fine points of law. The law is for lawyers to discuss. Our obligation is to provide to people an income by which they can maintain themselves. That is our obligation.

Author: What information should the woman take with her to her appointment in order to avoid wasting both her own time and that of the DHSS?

DHSS: Here again it depends on the circumstances. For example, if she has children, she should bring her Child Benefit book, and, if in the long term she intends going for an Action, she should bring their Birth Certificates. We would also want proof that she is married, so she should bring her Marriage Certificate. If she has any assets she should bring any papers relating to those assets. If she is buying her house, we would want to see the Mortgage Papers, so that we could calculate the housing requirements as we call it, i.e. the amount of allowance for, if you like, rent. The information required varies from person to person, but the rules of Supplementary Benefit are that it is up to the claimant to provide verification of the statement he or she makes. Now, to that end the claimant should bring everything she thinks will be needed. After that anything that has been overlooked we can ask for. Basically we would hope that the person would bring in as much as possible to allow us to authenticate her claim at the very outset. One of the problems that arises from lack of verification is that we might not be able to calculate her proper entitlement. A payment could be issued that night which might be for less than her proper entitlement.

Author: It would seem to me that the most difficult thing for her to prove at the outset would be that she was separated.

DHSS: Well, that can't always be confirmed on the day the claim is made, but, to come back to the battered wife, she may be accompanied by a welfare worker. That's been the case in my experience. The welfare worker would then be able to verify her statement. We would not be looking for evidence of assault. We are dealing with her within the category of separated or deserted wives. However, it has to be borne in mind that not every separated wife will be accompanied by a welfare worker. But in any case it is our practice to write to the husband asking him for his side of the story. We are required to establish the facts of each case as far as is possible.

Author: What information in the shape of leaflets and the like are available to the woman from the DHSS? How should she go about getting them?

DHSS: Her local DHSS office will have all the leaflets the woman will require, but having said this, it is a bit of an oversimplification. It is literally true, but if a woman goes in to pick up leaflets, she has to know what leaflets to get. Not everybody knows exactly which leaflets they are looking for. The best thing for a woman to do in these circumstances is to write to or call at her local office, give her details and say: 'These are my circumstances. Can you provide me with the range of leaflets which cover the Benefits to which you think I would be entitled?' Her circumstances would determine the range of leaflets that went out to her.

Alternatively, the woman simply might want to write to her local office, saying: 'Will you tell me what's available and what I should do?' She then could receive by return a letter, probably including a range of leaflets. Again she might be invited to call at the office and in some circumstances she might be interviewed at her home. There is no doubt that the personal interview is by far the best way of giving and obtaining information.

There is a variety of ways it can be dealt with, but at the end of it all, whichever way she chooses to obtain the information, I would hope that the woman would know all the Benefits to which she was properly entitled at that point in time, together with the appropriate Benefits should her circumstances change. For example, if she went back to full-time work, there is the possibility she might become entitled to Family Income Supplement.

That's how I'd like to see it work anyway.

Author: So really the DHSS is there as a strong financial help and they will make it their business to make as much money as possible available to that woman, that is all the Benefits to which she is entitled?

DHSS: Certainly. That's our prime purpose. Supplementary Benefit is intended to provide people with an income which will properly meet their requirements. The DHSS aim in a wider sense is to ensure that everybody has all the Benefits to which they are entitled, and of course, in addition to ensuring that a person's financial circumstances are taken care of, we do try to give advice and information.

Author: Such as advising the woman to see a lawyer, as you mentioned earlier?

DHSS: Yes.

Author: If she hadn't seen a Social Worker, then would you advise her to get in touch with one?

DHSS: Yes, we would do that where appropriate. We would offer any advice we considered appropriate to the situation.

Author: If she had nowhere to go and you knew there was a local branch of Women's Aid would you advise her to go there?

DHSS: We would certainly make her aware that the organisation existed. Our purpose is primarily to provide people with all the money they require, and secondly with all the information they require. Our main directive is to pay Benefits, but after that we will give as much welfare advice as we can to help a person to make the decision as to the next move. We will not make decisions for people, but if we are approached, then we will give advice and information, whether it be to go to see a Social Worker or the Housing Department or any other agency which might be able to help.

Statement from Scottish Women's Aid
August 1983

Women's Aid is a charitable organisation which gives advice, support and refuge to battered women and their children. The first Women's Aid group started in Edinburgh in 1973 and we have expanded over the years, to the extent that there are now 27 Women's Aid groups in Scotland, stretching from Shetland in the North to Dumfries in the South. In addition, the coordinating organisation, Scottish Women's Aid, was established in 1976. As well as coordinating the work of local groups, Scottish Women's Aid is responsible for setting up new groups and for publicising the problem of domestic violence nationally.

Each year literally thousands of women in Scotland are battered by the men they live with. During 1982/83 over 7,000 women in Scotland alone approached Women's Aid for help. Any woman living with a man can be battered. That is, she may be subjected to being beaten while pregnant, burned, kicked, not allowed out of the house, not given any money and generally humiliated and degraded. Women come to us for help from all social backgrounds and of all ages. In short, women are battered regardless of class, colour or creed.

Many women, by the time they come to us, are completely lacking in self-confidence and self-esteem having been continually told by their men that they are inadequate, useless, ugly and so on. Our most important task, therefore, is to help women regain their self-confidence and to learn to value themselves as people in their own right.

The help we offer is based on the following aims:

— To provide temporary refuge to battered women and their children and to offer support and advice to any such women whether or not they require refuge.
— To help the women to determine their own futures whether this involves returning home or starting a new life elsewhere.
— To care for the emotional and educational needs of the children involved.
— To offer support and assistance to women and children who have left the refuge.
— To encourage research into the causes, the prevention and relief of the suffering of such harassment.
—To educate and inform the public and professional bodies about the nature and extent of domestic violence.

Some women who come to us for help decide to stay in a Women's Aid refuge. Refuges are safe houses in which women can stay with their children for as long as they need. The refuge provides an atmosphere of safety and support in which a woman can decide, free of pressure, what action she wishes to take. This might be to return to her man or it might be to start a new life for herself and her children. We try never to refuse women who ask for refuge. If one refuge is full then we will try and find her a space in another refuge.

The refuges are run on a 'self-help' basis. This means that there is no warden and the women living in the refuges make their own decisions about how they want to organise cooking and cleaning. The women who come to the refuges come from a cross section of society. Many of them have had doubts before coming to the refuge about the 'kind of women' they will be sharing with, or the difficulties which they feel there might be in sharing with other people. We usually find that, because the women have been through similar experiences, they give each other tremendous support.

A woman coming to us for help does not need to require refuge. We give advice and support to women in our offices, over the phone or in a woman's own home, depending on a woman's own preference. The help we offer can include:—

— giving information about social security, housing and law with regard to battered women.

— helping women through the maze of appointments and dealings with the DHSS, Housing Departments and Lawyers.

All enquiries are treated in confidence and women can remain anonymous if they choose.

In April, 1982, the first refuge for Asian women in Scotland was opened. Situated in Strathclyde, it is open to Asian women from all over Scotland. The refuge can accommodate up to five women and their children. Not only can the Women's Aid group offer accommodation and the benefits of group support, but also they can provide interpreters to help women approaching housing departments and other agencies. This new initiative by Women's Aid is a much needed one as, until now, any Asian woman abused by her husband, unable to speak much English and unfamiliar with the workings of official bodies, had almost nowhere to turn for help.

You may wish to approach Women's Aid for information or for help— all enquiries will be treated in confidence.

— For general information on the work of Women's Aid and to contact groups in other areas: Scottish Women's Aid, 11 St. Colme Street, Edinburgh. 031-225 8011

—Asian Women's Refuge: Gryffe Women's Aid, Room 8, Old Community Centre, The Cross, Kilmacolm. Kilmacolm 2529

Edinburgh and Lothian Women's Aid
(Interviewed at Women's Health Fair, 28 May 1983)

Author: Can you tell me, first of all, what Women's Aid offers in the way of help to a battered woman?

Worker: Well, basically, Women's Aid offers advice, support and refuge for battered women and their children. Usually, when a woman first approaches Women's Aid for help, she will be counselled, possibly by someone who has suffered domestic violence herself, and given the relevant information she requires to make a decision about what to do next. We give advice on welfare benefits, the law, housing and so on, and explain the various options open to someone in her circumstances. Whatever the woman decided to do, we would help her achieve it. She might decide that she wanted to come into one of our refuges, which provide safe, temporary accommodation at secret addresses. Once in the refuge, she might decide to seek re-housing for herself and her children, and we would help her with that in any way we could.

Author: If the woman had to go to the Housing Department, or the DHSS, or to see a solicitor, would you go with her?

Worker: Yes, if she wanted us to. We have sympathetic solicitors with whom we deal regularly, and to whom we can refer women.

Author: Would Legal Aid be available to a battered woman?

Worker: Yes, if the woman was on supplementary benefit, or had a low income, all her legal costs would be covered by Legal Aid.

Author: Would you push the battered woman either way in her decision making?

Worker: No, absolutely not. The woman has to make her own decision. All we do is provide the relevant information and, once she has that information, the woman has to make her own mind up. We wouldn't blame a woman who chose to go back to her husband, because we can understand why women go back.

Author: What would you do about a woman who didn't want to leave her husband, but had simply come to talk to you about her position? I've heard from one woman who approached a Women's Aid group and was told they couldn't give her any help unless she decided to leave. She definitely had to make a decision to leave before they would help her.

Worker: Well, if she simply wanted advice and someone to talk to, we would always offer that, virtually on a 24 hour basis. We have an 'on call' service so women can get help at weekends and during the night when the offices are closed. If a woman only wanted information and advice, perhaps to keep in touch to discuss how things were going, we'd certainly speak to her whenever she wanted. We do realise that it's a very major step for a woman to actually leave home, expecially if she's got children, and it takes a great deal of courage. Very often, women need to think about it for a long time before they can make the break. We would never refuse to offer support and advice to someone who hadn't made up her mind to leave.

Author: If a woman decided to come into one of your refuges, what could she expect?

Worker: The houses we have for refuges are usually ordinary family houses, nothing special in any way. There would perhaps be three families staying in a three bedroomed house. The women living there with their children have to share the kitchen, bathroom and living room, but we try to ensure that each family has its own bedroom, so they have some privacy. There are no live-in staff. We run the refuges on 'self help' lines, as we believe that, once removed from a violent situation, battered women are perfectly capable of taking control of their own lives, with the support of other women who have had similar experiences to theirs. The women themselves decide how they are going to organise the housework and so on, and the workers and volunteers from Women's Aid only get involved occasionally when problems arise.

Author: What is a day like in the life of a refuge?

Worker: Well, it can be pretty chaotic! There's a larger than normal number of people for the size of the house, so it is fairly overcrowded. Breakfast and tea-time are probably the busiest times, with all the children to be fed, and only one kitchen. During the day, there is housework, washing and shopping to be done, as in any household. Sometimes the women in the refuge decide to shop and cook communally, as this can save money. In other cases, each cooks separately. It just depends on what they decide. Usually, there will be a visit from workers and volunteers from Women's Aid to make sure everything's going all right, and keep up to date with what's happening with each woman—has she had her appointment at the Housing Department yet, is she getting the right amount of money and so on. In spite of all the chaos, there is usually time, often at night after all the children are in bed, for the women to sit down and talk about their experiences. This is probably the most important thing we can offer battered women—the chance to see that they are not alone, and that what happened to them wasn't their fault.

Author: I feel that is a very important thing, that the women are able to talk to someone else who has been through a similar experience, so they feel they are not alone. It certainly would have helped me.

Worker: Yes, very often women come to us having completely lost their self-confidence as a result of the physical and mental batterings they have been subjected to. They blame themselves for the break up of their marriage, and even feel they must be to blame for being battered. Then they meet other women who have suffered the same experiences. They can see that these women are capable, confident and happy, so they know they can be like that too, in time. Later, they will be able to offer support and help themselves to the new women coming in.

Author: Does anything special happen in the evening?

Worker: There might be a house meeting once a week or once a fortnight. Some groups have them during the evening, some during the day. The idea is that all the women living in the refuge, and the workers and volunteers from Women's Aid, can get together to discuss any problems in the running of the house, or to talk about issues of concern to women generally. We sometimes have speakers along, and we talk about women's rights, rape, abortion, self-defence and so on.

Author: Whereabouts would your 'phone number, address etc. be available?

Worker: It would be available in the telephone directory, either under Women's Aid or Battered Women, or under the name of the town, such as 'Edinburgh Women's Aid'. The Scottish Women's Aid number is listed in all directories, and they would be able to give information on their nearest group to someone 'phoning in. There should be posters with the 'phone number and address up in various places such as local libraries, police stations, housing departments, social work departments and Citizens Advice Bureaux. The Samaritans are able to give a Women's Aid contact number, as are social workers, the police and Directory Enquiries.

Author: Speaking about the Highlands and Islands, there's no Women's Aid available there. Battered women have to come to the mainland to consult a solicitor to see the DHSS What kind of help would you like to see on the Islands?

Worker: Obviously, we'd like to see new local Women's Aid groups starting in areas where there is no provision at present. Scottish Women's Aid spends a lot of time trying to get new groups started. Ideally, there should be groups, with refuges, within easy reach of all women requiring this service.

Author: If a woman had come to you for help, then decided to return to her husband, what kind of help could you offer her?

Worker: If she wanted to keep in touch with us, perhaps by 'phoning, we could continue to give her any advice she required, and talk to her whenever she wanted. It can cause problems for women if their husbands find out they're still in contact with us, so we have to be quite careful in this kind of situation.

Author: Would you follow up a woman who's left the refuge and made a new life for herself? Would she still be able to turn to you for help?

Worker: Of course. We have found that, very often, women encounter major problems when they leave the refuge, such as loneliness, difficulties in coping financially and so on. We try to prepare them, as much as possible, for this before they leave. We do as much follow up as we can to try to alleviate these problems. We visit women in their new homes, try to put them in touch with other women we know who live near them and hope that they'll be able to offer each other mutual support. We often find that very strong friendships are formed in the refuge, which last after the women leave.

Author: What about help for the children?

Worker: We do try to do as much as we can for the children. Scottish Women's Aid has a National Children's Worker, whom the local groups can contact for ideas and advice about the children. In Edinburgh, we've had a 'Kidzade' group for some time. It meets on Saturday mornings in a local Community Centre and provides activities and outings for children currently in the refuges, and some who have been re-housed. In East Lothian, we have recently started a similar group, and a play group for under-fives is just starting in Edinburgh. In the past year we have been putting more time and thought into providing facilities for the children. It is a very difficult time for them as well, which shouldn't be forgotten.

Author: I think they could be the ones who are affected the most. Wouldn't you agree?

Worker: Well, they certainly can be affected quite severely. It's important to explain to them what's happening and why when they come to the refuge, so they're not made too confused and insecure. Often, women put off leaving violent men because they worry about the effects of leaving home on the children. We would always say that the effects on the children of violence in the home are much worse. Children usually enjoy living in the refuge once they settle down. There are always lots of other children to play with for one thing. Children are very resilient, and can put up with a lot of upheaval, as long as they understand what's going on, and are reassured that they are not going to be parted from their mother.

Author: How are Women's Aid groups funded?

Worker: All the local groups are funded individually. Scottish Women's Aid is funded by the Scottish Office, but has to fundraise 25% of their budget, which is quite difficult. Local groups are usually funded initially by Urban Aid grants and Manpower Services Commission temporary job schemes. Some of the longer established groups are funded by their Regional Councils. There was a COSLA (Convention of Scottish Local Authorities) Report in 1980 which suggested that Women's Aid groups should be funded 50% by central government, 25% by District Councils and 25% by Regional Councils. Unfortunately, this Report has been shelved, and nothing has been done about it.

The main problem is the uncertainty about future levels of funding. The grants received by local groups are determined annually, and are affected by local government spending cuts. The situation is most unsatisfactory, because the work we do is an essential service, and it is

vital that it continue. It should be available to every woman who needs
it.

Author: How much do you rely on voluntary help?

Worker: Very much. Without volunteers, we would simply not be able to
provide the same level of service. Volunteers are involved in all areas of
our work, running the offices, counselling, publicity work, fundraising,
working in the refuges, being 'on call'. We would prefer to be able to pay
everyone for the work they do for us, but our current level of funding
doesn't allow for that. Using volunteers allows us to provide the best
service for battered women that we can.

Author: Finally, do you have any advice for women who are being ill-
treated by their men and don't know what to do about it?

Worker: Yes—Contact your nearest Women's Aid group, find out what
your options are, and decide what you think will be best for yourself and
your children.

Solicitor (Scottish)
(interviewed May 1983)

Author: If I was a battered wife coming into your office today, how would
you best be able to help me?

Solicitor: Obviously, I'd find out what's involved in the matter—whether
you wanted to be separated from your husband, whether you wanted a
divorce, whether you were wanting just general advice as to what
position you're in and what steps you can take.

Author: You wouldn't push me in any direction?

Solicitor: No. It's not my job to do so. I would certainly, if the circumstances were such that I felt that it would be strongly detrimental for
you to, perhaps, remain in the situation, give strong advice one way. But
it's not my job to force the client. I can only give advice. Then it's up to
the client to make up her own mind, to give her instructions to me
based on my advice, and make use of my advice.

Author: Are there set steps that she would have to take having come to
you?

Solicitor: Well, obviously, first of all I'd have to find out what her problem
is. Now, if she's a battered wife and there are children involved and
she wants to resolve the situation, I would find out what the housing
situation is, because, obviously, that would have a big effect.

The *housing situation* is of prime importance because out of the house
there are obviously going to be great difficulties. You tend to find that
battered wives have no alternative accommodation available to them—
although possibly in some of the larger towns and cities there are

162

sheltered homes, special homes set up. So I'd find first of all some information about the existing accommodation—as to whether it was owned privately, or whether it was tenanted, and if tenanted, from which local authority, and if so, who is the tenant. And then, basically, that information would enable me to advise as to what steps we should take. If she is determined to go ahead, then court action is required to resolve the situation. So I would take her step by step through that.

Author: You mean court action against the husband?

Solicitor: Yes.

Author: In my experience, it's very rare that a wife will come up against this. All she really wants to go to a Solicitor for is to help her leave her situation. I've only heard of one case where the husband was actually jailed for six months. As soon as he got out he just beat her black and blue for having told the authorities in the first place. She was almost dead. And because of this fear, I don't think personally, that she'd want to prosecute. But if she did, what steps should she take?

Solicitor: Well, I wasn't so much talking in terms of criminal prosecution. I'm talking in terms of *Civil Action* to try to get Orders from Court to resolve her situation:

a) to get the tenancy in her name if it's not already in her name,

b) to get the husband out, and

c) to get an Order to stop him coming back. And hopefully at the same time getting some form of custody and alimentary award in favour of the wife and children, so that the wife's position is protected by Law. That doesn't, of course, mean that this is going to physically stop the husband coming back. But if he does come back, and he does act in breach of these Court Orders, then serious consequences, I'd say, would result.

Author: Is it true that there is now a new Law—the *Exclusion Order*?

Solicitor: That's right. It's an Act that was passed in 1981 which came into force on 1 September 1982—*The Matrimonial Homes (Family Protection) (Scotland) Act*. It was, in fact, based on the English legislation to try to resolve our matrimonial violence, although there do appear to be differences between the two systems.

Author: And what is the Exclusion Order?

Solicitor: Well, it's a system whereby one spouse—and the Law does not differentiate between male and female, male has the same right as female—can take an Order from Court excluding the other spouse from the home, if it can be shown that that Exclusion Order is necessary. I'll quote the Act:

'If it appears to the Court that the making of the Order is necessary for

the protection of the applicant or any child of the family from any
conduct or threatened or reasonably apprehended conduct of the non-
applicant spouse which would be seen as a danger to the physical or
mental health of the applicant or child.'

Author: Would the woman have to have proof?

Solicitor: Essential. There's no difference between this and any other
branch of the Law. Corroborative evidence would be required to
establish it.

Author: Would she have to have proof to come to you? I mean, say she
said she was a battered wife but she had no physical scars?

Solicitor: Simply because she has no physical scars that doesn't mean she's
not a battered wife. Most of my battered wives—if I can describe them
as such—don't have scars. But there are ways and means of getting
evidence: from neighbours, from medical evidence, hospital reports,
occasions police have been called to the house. There are various ways
and means in which statements can be obtained. Just because a wife
does not show the physical effects of the assault—and there may be no
other parties to the assault—it doesn't necessarily mean that she does
not have a case.

Author: In my case, I took five years' worth of diaries to a Solicitor. They
weren't shown as evidence, but the very fact that I had them helped me
obtain my divorce. This was in England. They helped me prove I was a
battered wife.

Solicitor: I don't think you would find that acceptable in Scotland. It is
not—how shall we say?—corroboration of your allegations of these
assaults taking place. But what possibly might happen—I don't know
what happened with you, whether the police were called out?

Author: No.

Solicitor: . . . or you had to go to your doctor, or things like that. This is
something that would be of assistance in pinning down dates—going to
the police and asking them if they were called to the house on such and
such an occasion, or going to the doctor and asking him for a report,
basically, of the incident that happened on such and such a date. But
really, you do require corroborative evidence.

Author: Necessarily from an outside party? I mean, what about the family
itself?

Solicitor: It can be anybody. There seems to be this view in the home that
it has to be somebody totally impartial. Well, that's just not correct. It
can be sister, brother, son, daughter, as long as they're of a reasonable
age and able to give a statement and, obviously, able to understand all
that is going on. Now, anybody and everybody is available for statement
purposes and for possible use in Court.

Author: Going again by my own case, which obviously I know a lot more about than anybody else's: there were no police involved other than for non-payment of fines by my husband for not paying his debts. It was more to do with the money side. The police were never called in because of violence. I thought they termed it as a 'domestic crisis'? In England, anyway?

Solicitor: Yes.

Author: None of the neighbours came in. They must have heard, but perhaps didn't want to be seen to have heard. They didn't want to interfere. They didn't want to get involved.

Solicitor: Yes.

Author: So there wasn't any outside help other than my parents and perhaps my sisters. That would have been enough?

Solicitor: Yes. Yes. That's quite valid. In fact, I would say in the majority of my cases of matrimonial disputes, the witnesses who corroborate the wife's allegation do come from within the family—mothers, brothers, sisters. So that, in the main, it's from the family unit that you would usually get your corroborative statements.

Author: Going back to this Exclusion Order—have I got it right, that with regard to a battered wife, if she's got children and she's contributed as much to the house as the husband has, if not more, can she bring in a doctor for corroborative evidence? Then bring in the police who issue the Certificate to be served on the husband?

Solicitor: No. Really the police don't have anything to do with that. The basis of the Exclusion Order is that the client will come to a Solicitor and say that she is a battered wife and explain the circumstances. An Action will then be raised either in the Court of Session, if it's a case for divorce proceedings, or, more normally, in the local Sheriff's Court combined with separation—and Action of Separation—or something like that. You would then present the Action in Court and seek to obtain from the Sheriff, or Judge in the Court of Session an Order initially on an interim basis suspending the husband's occupancy rights in the home and preventing him from returning there too. And that would cover the period right up to the final conclusion of the case which, in some cases, can take months, years. So you can seek an Interim Order very quickly after raising the initial Action.

In this connection, most people do require Legal Aid. Fortunately— and I don't have the experience of very many other Legal Aid Committees—in this Sheriffdom we work a very good system where we can obtain, in an emergency, a Legal Aid Certificate very rapidly for these types of Actions. Normally, say within a week, possibly quicker, of my client coming in, we can have an Action in Court for an Interim

Order suspending the husband's rights to occupy the matrimonial home.

Author: Once having left—the wife and children I mean—is it possible to pursue maintenance? Is it a solicitor who would do that?

Solicitor: Yes. For many people in these circumstances when they've had to leave the matrimonial home, the husband will probably refuse to pay, so that the wife will be receiving Supplementary Benefit. Therefore, what will happen is that the Department of Social Security will encourage the wife to approach a Solicitor to get some form of alimentary award, so that they can make use of this to obtain money for the husband; so that in effect, the State is not maintaining the children. The husband, through the DHSS, will be made to fulfil his obligations to his family.

Author: What if he still refuses to pay?

Solicitor: Well, if we have a Court Order, there are various steps that can be taken. Non-payment of alimony is one of the few civil matters through which you can still go to prison in Scotland. It goes back to 1882 and it is still valid. If a husband maliciously, deliberately, refuses to pay alimony payments, then a Court can order that he spends up to six weeks in prison at any one time. And this is a continuing thing. If he continues with it, the Court can make a fresh Order. But normally, if the husband is working there are ways of getting money out of him by Arrestment. I think the English Law calls it Attachment. A Sheriff's Officer will simply serve a copy of the Court Order on his Employer which freezes the husband's wages. And so the husband has to adopt a reasonable attitude at that time or else he'll get no money himself.

Author: Finally, does the Law differ in any way on the Scottish islands? It's obviously that much more difficult to get help there. You have to come on to the mainland to consult the DHSS and a Solicitor. Would these women be equally accepted? Would you be sympathetic?

Solicitor: There's absolutely no distinction one way or the other. I, quite honestly, couldn't care less where my client comes from. There is absolutely no difference in the Law. It is certainly true that with being on the islands the Law shall we say is less accessible than it would be on the mainland. We ourselves have a branch office in the Western Isles, and we have found that our existence there has generated work. So it's quite clear that, in fact, many people who do not have access to a Solicitor will accept situations. This is where I think people living on islands are at a disadvantage in seeking help to combat the problems.

Prior to September 1982, the position was that with most tenants in a matrimonial dispute, the husband could order his wife out of the house and unfortunately, the wife had to go because, as tenant, he was in control of the situation. Under the terms of the new Act, a wife, if she's not tenant, still has rights to occupy the house, which are called *Occupancy Rights*. And the husband cannot now force his wife out of the house. If he does physically, shall we say eject her, she can go to the Court to get an Order to reinstate her back into the house. So the wife is now definitely in a stronger position. But once she's in the house, the matrimonal home, she's in there for good unless the husband can establish the reasons why she shouldn't be— a reverse of the battered wife situation. Certainly, I don't think many wives tend to appreciate that they now have a right to occupy the house, irrespective of who's tenant.

Author: He couldn't take steps just for the hell of it to get her evicted, could he?

Solicitor: Well, before someone can actually legally evict someone else that person has to get an order from Court. Now, he could apply to the Court for an Order seeking an eviction. But the wife can always seek legal advice and defend the Action on the basis that she, as the house is the matrimonial home, has Occupancy Rights in the house. And as long as the Court is satisfied that that is the situation with the wife, and the husband cannot show good reasons why the wife should be put out— such as her conduct being a threat to the health of the husband or indeed the children—then there's no way in which a Court would, in these circumstances, make out an Order evicting the wife. So that she has the right to remain in the house until the Court decides otherwise.

Domestic Violence
Statement from English Solicitor
August 1983

For many people contacting a Solicitor to discuss the very personal details of a relationship is a very big step. It is important for the Solicitor to realise that the decision to make the initial contact has come out of a very long period of thought and has taken a considerable amount of courage. For this reason, it is important for the Solicitor to respond by making the earliest possible appointment for the Client to visit the Office to discuss her problems.

The amount of ground covered in the first interview will depend upon the urgency required to deal with the problems of the Client. If the Client is in immediate danger it will be necessary to obtain all the information at one interview and to take immediate steps.

When discussing the problems with the Client she may be confused by the surroundings and embarrassed by the nature of the matter and it is up to the Solicitor to bring out the relevant information in a coherent and ordered sequence. This will not only help the Solicitor but will also make the Client see the problems more clearly.

The relevant information required is as follows:

1. Details of the marriage or length of the relationship if the parties are not married.
2. Number of children (if any).
3. Details of any current or past matrimonial proceedings with the same spouse.
4. The financial position of the parties.
5. Whether they are employed, the income, savings, living accommodation (Unless it is intended to make an immediate application for maintenance then only brief details need be obtained at this stage. The majority of the details can be dealt with at the second interview).
6. Details of the matrimonial violence—is there a long history of violence? Is the violence petty or serious? (Obviously, the violence is going to be serious to the Client and whatever the nature it is important to obtain full details so that the Court's reaction can be gauged in advance). It is then necessary to go into specific instances. As a general guideline the first occasion of violence, the most serious occasion and the most recent occasion are good instances to start with. In some cases there may have been no history of violence or perhaps one instance of a serious nature. There may also be cases where there has been no actual violence but there has been a serious threat which the Client believes is genuine and which has frightened her.

Domestic violence may not be limited to violence against the female partner but may extend to the children of the family. Similar remedies are available to prevent violence or threats of violence against the child or children of the family as are available to the Wife.

When the Solicitor is in possession of all of the relevant facts he should be able to appreciate the type of problem the Client has, the reason why the Client has come to his Office and should have a good idea of the most suitable remedy for the Client.

There are probably three categories into which most Clients would fall:

1. A relationship where there has been habitual violence. This has an accumulative affect on the Client who has reached breaking point and has then come to see you.
2. A relationship with habitual violence where other factors have contributed to the breakdown of the relationship.
3. A relationship without previous violence where one incident or a very serious threat has caused the Client to be very shocked. This is probably the most serious type and these are probably the matters in which an order for family protection or an injunction should be applied for.

168

Remedies
First and foremost it is entirely the Client's decision as to what steps to take. All the possibilities should be placed before the Client before she has to decide. However, in practice the Client is often confused or more often than not, they are not aware of the remedies available to them before they visit the Solicitor. They may need guidance on the best steps to take. Even when guidance is given they should be given time to consider the effects of the steps on them and their relationship with the man involved.

Short term remedies
If the Client feels there may be a chance for the marriage or in more extreme cases where the Client or child of the family is in or feels that they are in any danger of violence from the husband or boyfriend there are two possible steps:
1. *The Domestic Proceedings Magistrates Court Act 1978* Section 16 and Section 18—in serious cases applications may be made at the Magistrates Court *ex-parte* i.e. not on notice to the person being the defendant. These applications are made by the Solicitor and Client visiting the Applications Court at the local Magistrates Court as early as possible in the morning. The application must be supported by a statement made by the Client with details of the marriage and details of the violence or threats of violence which have been made against them or a child of the family. The application is before one Magistrate who will read through the statement and then the Solicitor will be asked to run over the statement with the Client and the Magistrate or Clerk will then ask additional questions. If the Magistrate is satisfied that an order should be granted the Court will grant an expedited order to last until the matter can be heard in open Court (probably two weeks). If the application showed:
a) That the respondent has used or threatened to use violence against the person of the applicant or a child of the family and
b) It is necessary for the protection of the applicant or a child of the family that an order should be made the Court may make one or both of the following orders:—
i) An order that the respondent shall not use or threaten to use violence against the person of the applicant.
ii) An order that the respondent shall not use or threaten to use violence against the person of a child of the family.
Where on an application the Court is satisfied that:
a) The respondent has used violence against the person of the applicant or a child of the family or
b) That the respondent has threatened to use violence against the person

of the applicant or child of the family and has used violence against some other person or

c) The respondent has in contravention of an order made under Section 16 threatened to use violence against the person of the applicant or a child of the family and that the applicant or child is in danger of being physically injured by the respondent (or would be in such danger if they were to enter the matrimonial home) the Court may make one or both of the following orders:

1. An order requiring the respondent to leave the matrimonial home.
2. An order prohibiting the respondent from entering the matrimonial home.

If such an order is made the Court may add that the respondent should allow the applicant to enter and remain in the home.

An expedited order will not take effect until it is served on the respondent and it will cease to have effect on the first of the following:—

a) Twenty-eight days from the date of the order.
b) The date of the full hearing.

The Court may also include in the order provision that the respondent will not cause or incite any third person to use or threaten to use violence against the applicant or the child.

Also if the Court is satisfied on the granting of the order that the respondent has physically injured the applicant or the child and is likely to do so again the Court may attach a power of arrest to the order under Section 18 of this Act. This will allow a Constable to arrest without warrant if he suspects a breach of the order.

I must point out that the Magistrates are reluctant to exclude the respondent from the matrimonial home without allowing him a hearing and it will therefore be difficult to get such an order *ex-parte*.

At the same time as making an application for one or both of the above orders it is possible to make an application for a maintenance order for oneself and a child or children of the family under Section 2 of the same Act.

NB: The domestic Proceedings and Magistrates Court Act 1978 does not apply to non-married couples.

An order under Section 16 of the DPMCA will last for twelve months.

2. *The Domestic Violence and Proceedings Act 1976*

These proceedings can be begun in the High Court or County Court and there is no need to bring up a proceedings before applying for the injunction under this Act. Previously, with a Matrimonial Homes Act 1967 other proceedings e.g. divorce or judicial separation had to be begun before the injunction could be applied for.

A CRYING GAME

An originating application to the Court for the District where the applicant or respondent resides or where the matrimonial home is should be made. This is to enable powers of arrest to be enforced.

Applications must be served on the respondent at least four clear days before the return date (the hearing).

In urgent matters the application may be heard *ex-parte* although these applications should be the exception rather than the rule. A practice direction indicated as follows:—

'*Ex-parte* applications should not be made or granted, unless there is a real immediate danger of serious injury or irreparable damage'.

On *ex-parte* applications it is unusual to get an order to exclude the respondent from the home unless there are exceptional circumstances. Solicitors have been warned by the Courts that frivolous applications may result in them being personally liable for costs.

An Affidavit sworn by the applicant must accompany the application or be handed in when making the *ex-parte* application in person with a copy for service on the respondent.

Hearings will be before a Judge in Chambers and orders may be made for:
a) Provision restraining the other party to the marriage from molesting the applicant;
b) A provision restraining the other party from molesting a child living with the applicant;
c) A provision excluding the other party from the matrimonial home or part of it;
d) A provision requiring the other party to permit the applicant to enter and remain in the matrimonial home or part of it.
NB: This Act does apply to persons living together as man and wife.

It should be noted that the remedy under this Act is intended to be short term only and should not last more than a few months to allow the parties to make alternative arrangements and to commence other proceedings or effect a reconciliation. Any person in breach of an injunction is in contempt of Court which is punishable by a fine or imprisonment.

If the respondent is to be committed for contempt then an application with an Affidavit must be made to the County Court and copies served on the respondent. The application will be heard by a Judge and enforced by the County Court Bailiff. This process takes time! In addition, it can only be enforced by civil authorities and not by the Police.

It is therefore better to have a power of arrest attached to the injunction and this may be granted if the Judge is satisfied on the original application that the respondent has caused actual bodily harm to the applicant or a child of the family as the case may be and that he is likely to do so again.

Injunctions of this type may be applied for when other proceedings are pending i.e. ancillary to these proceedings but only where the nature of the proceedings bears some resemblance to the nature of the proceedings i.e. injunctions may be granted in divorce, adultery or judicial separation proceedings but not on an application for variation of maintenance payments or such similar application.

Both 1 and 2 are short term remedies and should be considered as such. The processes can be abused and the County Court in particular, as can be seen from the practice direction, has not taken kindly to this abuse. The applications under these Acts must not be frivolous and should only be made where it is necessary to obtain an immediate remedy.

Long term remedies
1. *Divorce.*

There is only one ground for divorce—'irretrievable breakdown of the marriage'. This can be proved by five facts. The relevant fact in cases of matrimonial violence is Section 1(2) (B) of the Matrimonial Causes Act 1973— 'that the respondent has behaved in such a way that the petitioner cannot reasonably be expected to live with the respondent'.

The question is whether, having regard to the behaviour of the respondent, it is reasonable to expect the petitioner to go on living with the respondent.

Procedure—the petition is prepared by the Solicitor setting out the matrimonial details and facts of unreasonable behaviour. The petition goes on to request dissolution of the marriage and ancillary relief and costs. Unfortunately, the Courts are very busy and there are procedural delays. The course of the proceedings also depend on the co-operation received from the respondent in completing the form of acknowledgement of service which states whether he will wish to defend the divorce or question the costs or take issue on custody or access of children or ancillary relief. A divorce taking the normal course which is undefended is likely to take between five and seven months. The ancillary relief which is normally dealt with after the divorce itself relates to the division of the property and the final maintenance settlement. This may take an additional six to twelve months, or possibly even longer, depending on the attitude of the parties. However, during this period, the petitioner may obtain maintenance pending suit for the period of the proceedings.

Obviously, this is the most definite end to a marriage. Not only does it put an end to the relationship, but it also divides the matrimonial assets and deals with the question of children. It may be necessary to take a short term step first and then apply for a divorce.

NB: It is not possible to apply for a divorce within the first three years of marriage unless the petitioner can show that there has been some extreme hardship or there have been some incidents of extreme depravity. In the past it was very difficult to prove either of these facts and there were very few petitions allowed through in the first three years of marriage. However, the Courts have become a little more lenient towards the applications.

2. *Judicial separation.*
This is not as final as divorce. It may be used if the parties have some religious objections to divorce or simply do not want a divorce. The grounds are the same as divorce but a party may present a petition without leave of the Court within three years of the marriage.

3. *Separation agreement.*
This is an agreement between the parties to the marriage. It can contain virtually any clause relating to the behaviour of the parties, division of the property, agreement as to children, although there are obviously some clauses which, by precedent, have been deemed not to be effective. There are no Court proceedings involved with a separation agreement and this type of agreement should only be entered into if the parties are on good terms and do not wish to have a divorce.

Legal Aid
The purpose of Legal Aid is not to provide free legal services but to enable people who cannot afford legal advice to obtain this. This may sound a contradiciton but there is a statutory charge which the Law Society (Legal Aid Fund) has over any money or property recovered as a result of proceedings. This will not apply where costs are awarded against the other party as the Legal Aid costs will then be paid by the other party. The statutory charge will not be enforced if this is likely to cause hardship and the minimum levels of property and money which can be recovered or which will not be subject to this charge.

Basically Legal Aid is available to anyone with a disposable income of under £4,400 per year and/or a disposable capital of no more than £2,750. The contribution which the Client has to pay towards Legal Aid is calculated on a sliding scale depending upon the Client's income. Disposable income is the net income after the deduction of income tax, national insurance contributions and also after making an allowance for any dependent spouse, children or other relatives in accordance with the Law Society's scale. Obviously the Solicitor would advise on the availability of Legal Aid at the time of the first appointment.

Legal Aid is available for proceedings under the DPMCA 1978 and the

DVMPA 1976 and an emergency certificate may be obtained to allow immediate representation. This can be obtained by making a telephone call to the local Legal Aid Office, who, after a brief explanation of the facts, will confirm that Legal Aid is available for the emergency applications for Family Protection Orders or injunctions.

No Legal Aid is available in respect of completing and filing a divorce petition and the conduct of the divorce (unless the divorce is defended which is most unusual). However, legal advice and assistance under the Law Society green form scheme is available. Basically this allows the Client to take initial advice from a Solicitor who points the Client in the correct direction and assists in the drafting of a petition and on the relevant steps to take. The costs which a Solicitor can recover under this scheme at present are limited to £75 which includes any VAT and disbursements. It is possible to obtain an extension to the certificate providing that reasonable grounds can be shown to the Law Society. The position regarding judicial separation and separation agreement is similar, in that legal advice and assistance can be given under the green form but a Legal Aid certificate is not available.

Legal advice and assistance under the green form scheme is available on any matter, but again the availability depends upon the means of the Client at the time of filling in the green form.

Housing position

There is a possibility that a wife may get sole possession of the matrimonial home under the short term provisions provided for in the DVMPA 1976 or the DPMCA 1978, but there are still the longer term questions to consider.

If the wife has been forced to leave the matrimonial home and does not intend to, or is not in a position to apply for an injunction or a family protection order with an accompanying order to regain possession of the house, then she may be able to persuade the Local Authority to re-house her in a flat or house, as they are under a duty to provide accommodation for anyone who is unintentionally homeless under the Housing (Homeless Persons) Act 1977. However, different Authorities interpret 'unintentionally' in different ways and there may be some considerable difficulty experienced by a Client if the Local Authority is short on housing facilities or there is a long waiting list.

Private rented property may be available and if the Client is on Supplementary Benefit the rent (providing that this is reasonable) will be paid by an addition to the ordinary allowance.

If the wife leaves the matrimonial home she will in no way lose her rights in the property.

Unfortunately, the provision of accommodation for both parties is the most difficult issue in a matrimonial split-up and is not a question which can be solved overnight. An order under the DVMPA or the DPMCA is only short term and the longer term settlement will be dealt with by the Court in the ancillary proceedings which, I have already said, may take well over twelve months.

DHSS and benefits available.

If the Client is working, she may be entitled to Family Income Supplement if her income is low. The children will be entitled to free school meals and she will be entitled to other benefits such as help with her rates, rent, electricity and free dental treatment etc.

If the Client is not working, she will be able to receive Unemployment or Supplementary Benefit. If she is in receipt of Supplementary Benefit, this will include provision for her rent. She will also be entitled, as will any children living with her, to all the benefits mentioned above and many others which are available from the DHSS.

The benefits are only aimed to keep a family at a subsistence level.

The DHSS require a wife to apply for maintenance from her husband for herself and the children (if any), if the husband is in a position to pay for maintenance. Obviously, there is no point in applying for an order for maintenance if the husband is out of work or if he is on a low income which is likely to only support himself. An application can be made for maintenance under the DPMCA 1978 Section 2. This is probably the quickest and simplest way of applying for maintenance.

In addition to these benefits the wife should consider her tax position especially if she is earning as she will be entitled to an increased allowance as a single parent family which will increase her allowance to the married man's allowance.

Generally, the Solicitor should offer basic advice on the benefits available and should then advise the Client to go and speak to the Department of Health and Social Security direct and also to go and speak to the Inland Revenue direct. The benefits from the DHSS can be obtained quite quickly and a phone call from the Solicitor will probably ease the Client's application through.

Basic Aims in dealing with a case of Matrimonial Violence

The aim of the Solicitor must be to get the Client to discuss the whole of the matter as fully as possible so that he can obtain the whole picture.

The Solicitor must then go on to advise what steps are available to the wife or girlfriend with regard to:

1. Accommodation.
2. Preventing the recurrence of the violence.
3. Maintenance.
4. Ending the relationship (if this is required).

It is important to remember that in very serious cases it is possible to act very quickly on all of the above matters and where the case merits this type of action every assistance should be given.

It is unfortunate, due to the large number of cases placing a heavy burden on the Court system, that matrimonial matters take so long to proceed through the Courts. As I have indicated, it is possible to act quickly in emergencies where a wife or child are at risk of being physically harmed. The family protection order and injunction offer short term remedies only and if the relationship is to be ended, the long term process must be gone through. The divorce itself is relatively easy provided that it is undefended and there is no dispute concerning the custody of the children. The majority of the time is taken up sorting out the ancillary matters relating to finance and the matrimonial home over which there is usually a wide divergence of opinions between the parties and on which it is not usually easy to reach an early settlement.

GP
(interviewed 14 June 1983)

Author: If a woman came into your surgery and told you she was a battered wife, what help or advice would you give her?

GP: First of all I would treat her injuries (if any), then in a case like this I would ask the woman a lot of questions about the violence that had taken place. I would also write down everything she said—what happened, when the events took place etc.—together with a detailed list of her injuries. This is so that there would be a medical record of the assault or assaults, in case at some point in the future I was asked for details by, for example, police or solicitors, if the woman decided to press charges against her husband, or if she decides to go to Court to take out an Action against him for divorce and maintenance. However, to go back to the first part of your question, it is rare, certainly in my experience, for a woman to admit straight out to her GP that she is being beaten by her husband.

Author: If a woman came into your surgery on a pretext of something else being wrong with her and you suspected that her husband was being violent towards her, what would you do?

GP: This is in fact what usually happens. Some patients, particularly women, do present their symptoms in such a way that the doctor does feel that they might have some other reason for coming. Women often come into the surgery and complain about headaches or depression (these are the most common), when really there is an underlying cause for their symptoms that they would like to discuss. In a case such as this I think my function first of all is to ask questions that are directed in such a way as to get the woman to admit to the underlying problem that is bothering her, and secondly to encourage her to talk about it. I would probe to try to get a true picture of her marriage, to find out if the couple had problems with money, sex, bad housing and so on. I would try to find out what the woman herself wanted to do about her situation. My main function, as I see it, is to provide a sympathetic ear. I would advise the woman only if and when she asked me.

Author: What sort of advice would you give, if asked?

GP: I think the main thing to do is to get the woman to look at herself and her situation and to ask herself what she wants to do about it. She, and she alone, must decide what she wants from then on.

As for advice—if she had decided to leave her violent husband, I would put her in touch with a Social Worker and I would suggest she went to see a Solicitor and the Housing Department (if necessary). If the degree of battering was extremely severe, I would suggest she contacted the police.

In the past I have been able to be of some practical help to a battered wife in so much as I helped to get her rehoused so that her violent husband would not be able to find her. I would do this sort of thing again if it were possible.

If a woman wanted to leave her husband but had nowhere to go and no support then I might suggest she contacted Women's Aid.

Author: Would you keep a busy surgery waiting while you talked to the woman about her problems?

GP: Yes. If I think any of my patients has a serious problem they wish to discuss, then I do not hesitate to keep the rest of my surgery waiting. As I said, providing a sympathetic ear at the time it is required, is all important. However, if the woman wished to see me again to discuss her problems further, I would tell her to ask the receptionist for a fifteen-minute appointment rather than a normal one.

Author: In the case of a battered wife, would you speak to the husband about what he was doing or would you go to see him?

GP: I certainly would not go to see him, but if he was a patient who was known to me, then I might ask him to come into the surgery to see me and I would speak to him there. I would try to discuss the situation with him and try to find out the reasons for his behaviour.

I am very wary of going to a house where an altercation has taken place, as I do not want to be called upon to act as mediator between husband and wife. It has happened to me in the past and what happens is that both husband and wife try to involve the doctor in the quarrel. This causes difficulties all round.

Author: If the woman remains in the violent marriage, would you inform other bodies (without telling her) so that they could keep an eye on the situation?

GP: I would not involve other bodies, for example the Social Worker, directly in the woman's own case, unless the woman asked me to, but if the woman had children I would probably have a word with the Health Visitor about the situation so that she could check up and ensure that the children were not being beaten up also.

Author: Do you encounter many cases of women who are being beaten up by their husbands?

GP: Well in my practice I don't come across that many, but I do encounter several cases where the man *and* the woman are violent towards one another, particularly after a joint drinking session at the weekend. Often the first I hear of a female patient of mine being battered is a referral from the Accident and Emergency Unit of the local hospital. It is interesting to note though that the problem occurs throughout all walks of life. There are battered wives in all classes of society; battered wives with husbands in manual jobs and battered wives with husbands in the professions; battered wives in all age groups. It does not occur only in working class households as many people believe.

Author: Finally, what is vaginismus and what would you do with a patient suffering from this complaint? Is the complaint particularly prevalent among battered wives?

GP: In my opinion vaginismus is basically a fear of sex, a fear of penetration. It is often caused by conditioning in a woman's past, e.g. an extremely repressed childhood, or it can occur in a woman who has been interfered with when she was a child, or in a woman who has been raped. It also often stems from a woman's ignorance of her own body and a resultant lack of feeling comfortable with her body.

It is a complaint which even the kindest, most patient husband in the world will find difficult to overcome. What happens is that when the husband attempts penetration, the wife's vaginal muscles contract and go into spasm, thus effectively blocking his entry. Any attempt by him to force his way further in will be extremely painful to the wife.

I would not say that the condition is any more prevalent in battered wives than it is in other women, but if vaginismus was present in a wife who had told me that she was being battered, then I would question her further about her marriage and in particular about how she saw her sexual relationship with her husband.

As to treatment—I would send the woman either to a gynaecologist or to the psycho-sexual counsellors at the Family Planning Clinic. They have the facilities and the specialised knowledge to help the woman to overcome her fear of penetration by getting her to use methods such as dilators to expand her vagina and to be relaxed about penetration. They will talk to the woman also about her body and how to overcome her ignorance of it and generally help her to become more relaxed about herself. There are also Sex Therapy classes where, amongst other things women are encouraged to examine their own genitals with mirrors in order to help themselves become more comfortable with and more knowledgeable of their own bodies.

Doctor working in sex therapy
(interviewed 28 June 1983)
This doctor was also asked to explain what is meant by the condition vaginismus.

Doctor: 'Classic' vaginismus is a completely involuntary contraction of the vaginal muscles which makes penetration difficult or impossible. This will include not only penetration during sexual intercourse, but also penetration by finger or tampon.

The condition can exist in women who are in other ways sexually responsive or even orgasmic. The cause of the condition is often unknown, although occasionally it may result from a painful experience such as rape or a traumatic gynaecological examination.

Vaginismus is often one reason why a marriage may not be consummated.

There are many other situations where a woman may tense her vaginal muscles making penetration difficult. This may be because she fears pain, or physical abuse, or simply because she doesn't want to have sexual intercourse with that particular man. In the past her sexual experiences may have been perfectly successful. A woman like this cannot be said to have 'classic' vaginismus.

Author: Can the condition be treated?

Doctor: Yes. Any woman can be taught voluntary control over these vaginal muscles through specialised exercises.

Author: How should a woman set about obtaining treatment?

Doctor: What usually happens is that a woman goes to her GP or Family Planning Clinic and mentions her worry that her marriage has not been properly consummated. She will then be examined. From there she will be referred to a sex therapist such as myself, although some GPs have

experience in the field of sex therapy and will treat the patient
themselves.

Author: Would you say vaginismus was more likely to occur in women
who have had sexually repressed childhoods?

Doctor: No. As I said earlier vaginismus is an isolated condition. It is an
involuntary reaction. In my experience women who have had repressed
childhoods are more likely to be generally sexually unresponsive, rather
than to have vaginismus. Women who have vaginismus are often very
sexual women. They want to have intercourse but can't.

Social Worker
(interviewed 19 May 1983)

Author: If I was a battered wife coming to you today, what would my
rights be or what help could I expect?

Social Worker: Well, the help that we would give you would be to advise
you where you could go for specialised help in the first place. We would
obviously have to talk to you to see exactly what you wanted to do in
the long run—whether you wanted to leave your husband, or whether
you wanted to stay with him.

Author: You wouldn't push me in either direction?

Social Worker: No, I don't think we could, because if you were coming to
us for help, then obviously you want something to happen, whether it is
a reconciliation, or to get out of the situation altogether.

Author: I would probably be confused in my own thoughts as well as to
what it was I really wanted, whether I actually did want to leave him
and all that entailed, i.e. starting a life of my own, or whether I just
wanted help within the marriage: help to cope and to try to get him to
go for help as well.

Social Worker: Yes, in that case we would have to discuss the ins and outs
of the case very thoroughly, obviously your emotional feelings. If you
felt that you wanted to make a go of it in the hope that your husband
would perhaps change, then we would try to put you in touch with the
nearest Marriage Guidance Council and we would try to talk to your
husband to explain that this was happening. We would tell him that his
wife is very upset about it, and that it is not fair to her. We would ask
him if he wanted it to stop, because a lot will depend on what he wants
as well.

Author: He may well decide that the marriage has come to an end and
that solves itself. But if he is not prepared to accept that violence is a
problem, which I doubt whether he would, what then?

Social Worker: This is of course a possibility, this is what happens. Well, then I think that you have to determine—right, I have had enough, I want out of the situation—and then it would be a case of do I want away from the home situation, or do I want my husband away from the situation? Either way, our advice would be to see a lawyer about your legal position. We would probably help you contact one who would advise you about your legal position and about Legal Aid.

Author: With it being such a major step, would the Social Worker be willing to go with me to the solicitor?

Social Worker: I think if you were really upset they would. I certainly think that if you were in a terrible state they would. Of course, the other thing that would be asked, which is always going to be asked, is have you involved the police? This will be asked by a lawyer as well as a Social Worker. Obviously, if you have been battered you will be asked if you have seen either the police or a doctor. If so, what does the doctor say?

Author: What if you have seen neither police nor doctor, and you have no evidence of bruising on you, but you still say that you were battered mentally and physically (it is a mental thing as well) and rape obviously comes into it?

Social Worker: Well, this is where it is slightly tricky. Again, a lawyer I think is the only person who can give you the legal angles to that, but if you are saying that you are mentally and physically assaulted, that you are raped, that you want out of the situation, then obviously you have got to find somewhere to go. The first thing a qualified Social Worker will ask is if you have got family or friends that you can go and stay with. If you haven't, then possibly they will try to put you in touch with a group for battered wives or some kind of refuge where you can stay, even if it is only just to sort yourself and your feelings out.

The legal side obviously has got to be dealt with by a qualified person; it is not up to the Social Worker, they couldn't do that. I think really in this role, a Social Worker's job is to help you talk through your own feelings, to try to help you make your own decisions and to put you in touch with people that can help you even further, e.g. DHSS, because there will probably be money problems and you will need help to pay a lawyer and to pay for somewhere to stay. From there it is up to you, once you get a breathing space, to decide yourself where you want to go, and you are probably more able to cope with it away from the situation.

Author: Does the position change if you have children?

Social Worker: If the children are obviously at risk and suffering then obviously it would change.

Author: If they are not actually suffering now, then my fear would be that they would be in the future, so my main concern would not be for myself, but for my children.

Social Worker: I think that some of the same standards would apply in that possibly you would need help to find somewhere to stay with your children, if you had got nowhere to go or no relatives you could go to. You would need legal advice and you would need money, and again I think that the main basics are those. If there was evidence that the children were also suffering, then probably the Social Worker would be quicker to step in to help you than if you were a single person, adult. People seen as adults should be able in some way to help themselves.

Author: Yes, it comes down to yourself in the end?

Social Worker: Yes. Whoever you talk to and whatever you do, the final decision has to be yours. I mean there is no question that anyone else can make those decisions for you. You are an adult.

How to Help Yourself
Janine Turner
People ask me how to live through hell and come out on the other side sane.

   'Who helped you?' they ask.
   'Who was your best friend?'
   'Me,' I say, simply.
   'You?' They are incredulous.
    'Yes. But who helped you through?'
   'Me,' I repeat. 'Me, me, me!'
And I share with them my secret—*How to Help Yourself.*

1. Ask Yourself these questions:
   Who am I?
   What am I?
   How am I physically?
   Where do I want to go?
   Do I need outside help?
   What do I want out of life?
   Come to terms with yourself.
   I asked myself these questions a lifetime ago.
   'Who am I?' I asked in a still, small voice.
   'I am a battered wife,' came back the reply.
   'I am a failure. A freak. No good to anyone, least of all myself. I feel depressed. Withdrawn. Afraid. Afraid of what? Of myself? Of myself.'
    I cried a little. Laughed a little. Cried a little more. Before going on. I

had to be honest with myself, and it hurt.

'What do I want to do with my life from now on?'

'I want more than anything to find myself. And yes, I need help. But who can show me the real Me, the Me locked away inside?'

'What do I want out of life?'

'Happiness. A home. Love. Children. I cannot survive the way I am. I am an emotional cripple.'

Having asked myself these questions and answered them, I had taken the first important step towards helping myself.

2. *Sit in front of a mirror. Look at yourself. Look at the face, the figure. You. Stare back. Become familiar. Be friends. Smile. Scowl. Pull faces. Relax. Accept yourself for who and what you are.*

'I am me,' say a few thousand times at your reflection.

'I AM ME!'

When I performed the same test, I found myself looking critically at my fuzzy greying hair.

'Oh, I wish I looked even a little like Farrah Fawcett,' I sighed, enviously.

My eyes sagged with bags. My mouth drooped into a double chin. My figure filled the mirror. I was a physical and emotional mess.

'I am. . . !'

Say it. Believe it. Accept it as a basis to work from, and decide how to improve it.

3. *Map out for yourself a way of life. Start now. Today is the first day of the rest of your life. Start at the top and work down. Visit the hairdressers, dentist, optician and doctor if necessary. Prepare the new you to meet the world.*

Buy at least one new thing, however trivial, and don't stint yourself. This is your day. Make the most of it.

Eat the right kind of food. Work out your danger periods and use them to pursue a hobby. Something new. Something you haven't tried before.

I have always loathed needlework—a button can still stay off for weeks—but when I wanted to stop snacking at night, I took up embroidery and tapestry. It worked! It took my mind off 'comfort food'. Gave me an ideal form of relaxation. The secret is to find something that works for you.

4. *Visualisation.*

Try to find a way of bringing out your positive side. Don't rely on someone else. Find from within yourself the resources to go out, to meet people, to talk and laugh naturally without fear of inhibitions getting in the way.

Stand up for yourself. You are you. Don't be ashamed of it. There is NOTHING to be ashamed of.

The colours red and black work for me. Don't ask me why! They just do. They are what I call my 'positive colours'. Somehow, wearing them gives me the confidence to talk, to write, to reach out and hold people's attention. To be Me. I am still sorting out the problem of shyness, of wanting to hold back, of catching myself making an excuse not to go out to meet someone. It isn't easy. You have to work at it, and keep working.

5. *Sit down and make a list of all the things you would really like to be able to do. Jot them down spontaneously. Don't try to think too hard about them, or to put them into any kind of order. When the list is complete— long or short, it doesn't matter—put beside each one the reasons why you haven't done it, or haven't felt able to do it. This is important in order to sort out your feelings. To analyse. To make a new start. To help yourself.*

My own list went something like this:

I would like to be able:	*I can't because:*
to go to a dance/party	I've always been odd. Different. I don't feel others will accept me. I am afraid of being Me.
to lose weight	I eat when I feel lonely. Diets are boring.
to visit the dentist	I know it will hurt. I have a hole in my tooth, but I am afraid of pain. Afraid of what the dentist will think of me cringing in his chair. I feel a failure.
to have a child	I am frightened of sex. To me, sex = rape. Sex is taboo. I feel I can live without it—but then, how can I have a child?
to drive a car	I've no confidence in myself. I am afraid to try something new. No nerve. No willpower to succeed.
to write a book	although I keep diaries and find it helps to write my thoughts down on paper, to write a book is to become noticed. I'm frightened of what people will think, I'm scared to push myself into the limelight.

My list proves I was afraid simply to be myself. Your fears may be very different. What will your list contain?

6. *Set yourself a task. Choose at random from YOUR list something that you would like to be able to do. This won't be easy. Up until this point,*

it has all been theory. This is your chance to put theory into practice. This is the real test. But you must stick with it. Don't give up now.

Brace yourself. Go out and face your particular giant. Your fear. Do it alone. It won't work if you lean on someone else. It will probably be the most positive step you take to help yourself.

Afterwards treat yourself to something special as a reward—you will have earned it. And don't talk at length about what you are about to do. Just do it.

I chose going to the dentist. It was hard. It is still a particular phobia of mine and I can still be physically sick at the thought of going. But it was something I had to do, so I made myself do it. It was five years since I had last been. I rang to make an appointment. I walked up and down past the door, down and up, up and down. I almost went home. Instead I walked quickly through the door and sat down in the dentist's chair. I was shaking. I was crying. I was sick. But I did it. The feeling of relief was enormous. Afterwards, I treated myself to the biggest cream cake I could find.

7. *Congratulations! If you have got this far you are doing well. Have a break for a while before going on, but not for too long. You don't want to lose the incentive to succeed. To help yourself.*

When you feel ready, take another item on your list. Play it through. Then another and so on, the target being to complete your list. Now, make a table of your accomplishments. If you like, put the date of success after every task. Write down how you felt, how you beat your fear of the unknown, how you helped yourself.

The first three items on *MY* list took a long time to complete; the final three even longer! But I did it and that is what matters. I succeeded. I helped myself.

After I had been to the dentist, I took steps to lose weight. I ignored conventional diets completely and took up jogging instead and a less likely candidate for jogging I have yet to meet! I jogged heavily, laboriously, painfully, around the park at six every morning so no-one would see me. I pushed myself, paced myself, until I could complete four rounds (about one mile). And I lost weight! Then I found I was actually enjoying this new experience, so it became a part of my life.

To get to go to a dance or party took slightly longer. I first found a job as a hairdresser's receptionist. I was chosen from fifty applicants which did wonders for my morale! People began to notice and comment on this new Me and from there I got invited to a dance. This was it! I sweated. I suffered agonies that night, but at the end of it, I was on an all-time high. I had danced my feet off. I had won.

Having a child meant an operation. I was considered to be infertile. I underwent tests and the verdict was blocked fallopian tubes. Fostering? Adoption? Mike and I considered both. Then an operation proved successful. Joanne was born, a child born of love.

I passed my driving test only last year, and it has opened out a whole new life for me. It means I can travel. I can be my own boss without having to rely on others.

I tried writing. Being open. Honest. Putting this new Me down on paper. This book is the fulfilment of that dream.

8. *Lastly some words of advice:*
a) *Be a listener.* Don't be so overwhelmed to find a friend that you bombard them with your life story. Concentrate on them. Learn from them. Be a friend. You will find that someone else's problems are often worse than your own.
b) *Don't pretend.* If someone mentions a book they have read, a film they have seen, *say* if you don't know what they are talking about. There is nothing worse than trying to hold a conversation with someone who says 'yes' all the time.
c) *Be still.* When you are in company, talking to someone else or simply 'being seen', don't be so selfconscious that you fidget persistently. I know even now I have to stop myself fiddling with my hair, scratching my nose, picking imaginary fluff from my skirt.

Do all your worrying in the mirror beforehand. See that your hair is tidy, your new dress fits well, tights unholed, and that you are wearing a pair of shoes that won't cripple you before your evening is over. Then go out and *be you.* Remember that you are as good as, if not better than, anyone else.
d) *Don't be afraid to say 'No'.* Practise saying it at home in front of the mirror first. Then say it to family and friends. When someone asks you to do something you don't really want to do, tell them 'No' honestly. Explain why not. Don't feel obligated.

9. One word of warning—don't do too much at once. Take it slowly. Come to terms with yourself gradually. If you cannot follow any of the pointers I have outlined, ask yourself why not? Examine your motives, your feelings. Try to understand them. Then try again and again until you succeed. Ease yourself into the new you.

10. Make up your mind to succeed and you will. I live by a kind of motto and it helps if I find life too hard, or tasks too difficult to cope with:
A man's reach should exceed his grasp else what's a heaven for?

(Browning)

Find a saying to suit yourself.

If you meet someone else who needs help, become their friend. They could probably use one. Share with them the secret of *How to Help Yourself.*